The Grunts

Charles R. Anderson

PRESIDIO PRESS · SAN RAFAEL · CALIFORNIA

THE GRUNTS

Charles R. Anderson

copyright © 1976

by

PRESIDIO PRESS
31 Pamaron Way
Novato, California 94947

Fourth Printing 1984

Library of Congress Catalog Card Number 76-4153
ISBN 0-89141-003-1

Book Design by Geri Davis

Illustrations by Cornelius Cole Smith, Jr.

Printed in the United States of America

DEDICATION

This book is for Sam,
and for
Chief, D. J., Red Mountain, Beck,
Day Tripper, Big Dipper,
L. C., Old Man, Hair,
Brother Books, Pooch, Whitey,
and all the rest.

Contents

Acknowledgements vii
Introduction ix
Vocabulary Note xiii

part one: The Tour

1. Hotel Twenty-Nine 19
2. Bravo-One Three 35
3. May Day 53
4. The Best Years of His Life 69
5. The Third Herd 85
6. Ho's Birthday 99
7. Moaning and Groaning 113
8. Hill 174 125
9. Hill of the Angels 141

part two: The World

10. Our World and *The World* 155
11. Preparation 167
12. Atrocities — Why? 175
13. "Take Care of Your Men" 187
14. Reactions 195

Epilogue

Acknowledgements

In the course of my own tour in Vietnam, I met several hundred persons whose actions and comments contributed in some measure to this book. However, I would like to cite in particular Bruce Williams, Herman Wimbush, George Webb, James Sloban, Hector Perez, Archie Morton III and Michael McCloskey for offering their own descriptions and interpretations of Vietnam. Special thanks is extended to Professor Charles C. Moskos, Jr. of Northwestern University who did so much to help this work across that broad gulf which separates written manuscripts from published books. I am further indebted to my manuscript typists of two cultures — Joyce Brown Duesing, Catherine Havelick, Nancie A. Wood and Kiyomi Sugawara.

Introduction

This book is an attempt to describe the Vietnam War as it was experienced by the individual infantryman, the grunt. This personal account of the war shares that purpose with several previous efforts. But in fulfilling its purpose this work moves in different directions than others, because it incorporates a different view of the experience of the Vietnam War. Earlier accounts have presented the war as a one-dimensional experience; only that which occurred in the war zone was recounted. This account, however, presents the Vietnam War as a two-dimensional experience. Both that which the participant did in the war zone and what he found on his return to America are examined. Such a definition of the total experience of the Vietnam War requires that the account make a radical change of focus, from the microcosmic to the macrocosmic. But that is a change of focus which must be made if the account is to be true to its purpose, for the experience it describes includes the same change of focus.

In experiencing the war and then his postwar hometown, the participant was forced to rapidly expand the focus of his action and concern from an environment small and concentrated to one large and diffuse. In Vietnam the infantryman could afford only to be concerned with survival and its related questions. The environment allowed no more. But back in America, where survival has a completely different definition, he could not afford to be concerned with only one issue. The home environment forced an expansion of perception and concern. Thus the total experience of the Vietnam War amounted to a forced move from a microcosm to a macrocosm. This account makes the same change of focus.

Existing accounts of the war concentrate on the microcosmic aspect of the experience — the war in Vietnam. The macrocosmic aspect — the readjustment to American society — has been largely ignored in spite of the fact that it was for many veterans as wrenching an experience as the war. Thus there persists an unbalanced understanding of what those who went to and returned from the war experienced. This account is an attempt to redress that imbalance.

Part One of this account details the actions of one U.S. Marine infantry company on a 58-day combat operation. All incidents happened as related. The events described are those encountered by only 160 men, though the adversity recounted is representative of that experienced by all grunts in Vietnam. The chronology of the account is interrupted by brief descriptions of what a few Americans far from the war were doing. The juxtaposition of grunts in Vietnam and civilians in America is used to illustrate how, to the former, the seemingly innocuous actions of their countrymen appeared at various times hilarious, absurd, maddening, even threatening — anything but normal or logical.

Part Two differs from Part One in two respects. First, the scope of analysis is much wider. Postwar and select prewar experiences of all the grunts, not only those of one infantry company, are examined against a background much larger than that of the war — American society of the late 1960s. Before they went to Vietnam, the grunts had a particular set of experiences which equipped them with certain expectations about war and one's return from it. But those who went to and returned from this war found that previous experience was poor preparation for what Vietnam and the American public presented them. Part Two also differs from Part One in that it manifests a conglomerate character. In addition to a consideration of the society which the grunts came from and returned to, there is presented in Part Two an investigation into those actions of the grunts which contributed nothing toward the accomplishment of their official mission in Vietnam. Herein is a discussion of the causation behind two such actions: atrocities against Vietnamese civilians and fraggings, the attempted murder of unit leaders by some of their troops. American troops in Vietnam displayed a very human mix of the admirable and the questionable. While there was heroism and compassion, there was also fear and indifference, cowardice and brutality.

Before this account begins, several persistent misconceptions should be countered in order that the overall experience of the war on the ground in Vietnam will be better understood. First, many distant observers believed during the war years — and somehow still believe — that American troops in Vietnam outnumbered their enemy. In fact, however, there were never more than one-fifth as many Americans in the field as the Viet Cong/ North Vietnamese Army. The organization of communist forces was such that their ratio of troops in the field to total personnel in uniform was much higher than that of the American force. Total field strength of the VC/NVA was usually estimated at 300,000 to a half million. In contrast, the American Military Assistance Command, Vietnam, was top-heavy with rear-echelon staff personnel, much more so than any previous military force America sent to war. The ratio of troops in the field to personnel in Vietnam was consistently between one to six and one to eight. Applying that ratio to the 540,000 Americans in uniform in Vietnam at the height of the American involvement, we find that only 67,000 to 90,000 were assigned to front-line combat units. Pushing that figure even lower was the normal attrition of personnel caused by malaria, rest and recreation leave, heat exhaustion and combat. Thus, there were never more than about 80,000 American ground troops actually looking for and fighting over 400,000 VC/NVA. The American force was of course augmented by the South Vietnamese Army, which numbered about 800,000 in 1969, but that force was for several reasons not nearly as effective as its size would indicate. While American grunts did enjoy certain advantages over their enemy, numerical superiority in the field was definitely not one of them.

Second, the great contrast between the war experience of troops in the field and that of rear-echelon staff and support personnel is still not appreciated among those who did not see the war. By the mid-1960s American military science had so developed that less than twenty percent of the personnel in the U.S. Military Assistance Command, Vietnam, were infantrymen. The majority were engaged in a myriad of support activities. Incredibly, for that majority life could be as secure and comfortable as it was for those assigned to a base in the States. In the rear-echelon bases there were all those things the troops in the field were denied. There were movies, free time, dry beds with clean sheets, mail and showers every day and plenty to eat and drink. And there were the clubs, the clubs with their air conditioners, pool tables, slot machines, floor shows, steak dinners and, "would you care to see the wine list, sir?" The comforts enjoyed by those in rear-echelon bases were a constant source of resentment for the grunts.

Finally, even among troops in the field, the adversity encountered was not uniform; time and region influenced the grunts' experience of war. The war in the hills of the northern provinces of South Vietnam, of which this is a partial description, was much different from the war in the rice paddies of the Mekong Delta region, or the war in the urban centers. And, the war in 1969 was almost as different from the war in 1965 as was the Vietnam War from the Korean War.

None of the incidents described herein is merely true to the spirit of the experience of Vietnam. All dates, place names, unit designations, and events in this account are factual. However, in accordance with the wishes of certain participants, or their survivors, all names have been changed.

Vocabulary Note

Like most wars, the Vietnam War provoked a vocabulary of its own. Many of the hundreds of words and phrases coined during the war appear in this book and require explanation.

After they had been in their branch of the military for awhile, the marines rarely referred to their organization as the Marine Corps. They preferred terms less officious and more descriptive of their experiences with the workings of the Corps. They decided on terms decidedly uncomplimentary — the *green machine*, the *crotch*, the *green weenie*, and *this green mother*.

In *the Nam*, the grunts spent most of their time in the *bush*, the field, far way from towns and cities. In the bush the grunts *humped*, walked, after two enemies, the *VC*, the Viet Cong, and the *NVA*, the North Vietnamese Army. In their humping after the VC and NVA, the grunts were sometimes assisted by the South Vietnamese Army, the Army of the Republic of Vietnam, *ARVN*, pronounced *arvin*. The humps and search and destroy operations carried out by the grunts were planned and supervised by high-ranking staff personnel and unit commanders, the *heavies*, of the military hierarchy. However, when the grunts said they were *busting heavies*, they were working hard, not doing anything to their commanders. Unlike most grunts, most heavies were *lifers*, they were making a career of military service.

The number *six* was the designation for the commander of any unit larger than a platoon, and was preceded by a codified term for a particular unit: *Bravo Six, Mustang Six*, etc. The term *Sky Six* was a slang designation for God. Unit commanders wanted their troops to carry out directives and missions *ASAP*, as soon as possible, and according to the *SOP*, standing operating procedure.

During both offensive and defensive operations the grunts occasionally encountered Vietnamese civilians. The Vietnamese were almost always referred to in the most derogatory terms — *gooks, gooners, zipper-heads* or *zips, slopes, dinks*, and *slant-eyes*. In contrast to the last term, *round-eyes* designated westerners.

Life in the bush was generally a *bummer*, an adverse experience, which was only rarely broken by the *bennies*, benefits like warm beer and letters from the *World*, the United States. When they appeared, the bennies were delivered by a *bird* or *chopper*, a helicopter. Whenever possible, the grunts *cut each other a hus*, did favors for each other, to relieve the adversity.

The grunts had much to fear in the bush. Some of the most common fears were of being wounded, being denied the bennies for several days, receiving *office hours*, and hearing about *Jody* back in the World. Office hours was an expedient form of dispensing punishment for minor violations of the Uniform Code of Military Justice. Jody was the guy who stole a grunt's girl friend back in the World while the latter was serving a tour in the war. The grunts' greatest fear, of course, was of being killed, the most common terms for which were *dinged, zapped, greased, blown away, caught his lunch*, and *bought the ranch*.

part one
The Tour

*It's a small war, God, but
it's the only one we've got.*

*anonymous, sign over chaplain's
bunker at Con Thien, 1967*

With America's newest war heating up in the mid-1960s, draft calls were raised and standards for volunteers were lowered. Existing training facilities were expanded; new camps and schools opened. By the summer of 1968, dozens of training camps and specialist schools were turning out thousands of troops and junior officers every month. They learned how to fly helicopters at Fort Rucker, Alabama; load napalm and bombs on fighters at Lackland Air Force Base, Texas; lead infantry platoons at Quantico, Virginia, and Fort Benning, Georgia; and drive tanks and trucks at Camp Pendleton, California. They were taught to cook mess hall food at Camp Lejeune, North Carolina; run an Army photographic lab at Fort Monmouth, New Jersey; fire aircraft carrier boilers at Norfolk, Virginia; treat combat wounds at Great Lakes, Illinois; conduct counter-guerilla warfare at Fort Bragg, North Carolina; and fly Phantom fighter-bombers at Pensacola, Florida. Their training complete, these new warriors were given thirty days leave before reporting to one of several military air terminals on the West Coast. There they boarded civilian jets, complete with in-flight meals and smiling stewardesses, for the flight to Da Nang or Saigon.

1

Hotel Twenty-Nine

Travis Air Force Base is about an hour-and-a-half drive up Interstate 80 from San Francisco. The highway roams over and between those low hills linking the Bay Area with California's vast agricultural interior. Tract housing creeps obscenely up some of the slopes. An occasional billboard claims too much of the view; one screams "Impeach Earl Warren!" To the west is that huge red sun falling into the Pacific. The reason they call it "Golden California" becomes obvious on this road at this time of day. Before it moves out of sight, the red ball turns everything a glowing, fluid gold — the rolling hills wearing a soft grassy mantle and a few clumps of trees and mounds of rocks; the highway, black most of the day; even the oncoming cars bearing natives in deep tans, outrageous colors, and — always — the sunglasses. You squint at the goldness of everything, but it's not like squinting at the glare of midday sun off a new snowfall — this feels good, warm, almost makes one desire sleep. So you squint to expose more of your eyelids to that golden warmth, and you want to stay — *goddam, you want to stay all of a sudden — did I really volunteer for this thing?*

Soon the gold ball leaves to tend to Hawaii, the thousands of mini-islands farther west, then on to that part of the planet misnamed the Far East. In *the Nam* the same gold ball drives the colonels and generals into their air-conditioned headquarters offices. It drives the supply *pogues* in the rear bases to their Coke machines and fans. And it drives the grunts into bunkers at fire support bases or into streams in the bush, the streams with their leeches and black water fever.

Signs come out of the dusk, reporting one's progress on the way to war:

... Fairfield 11, Sacramento 52 ... Fairfield 4, Sacramento 45 ... Welcome Fairfield Suisun ... Fairfield Beauty Academy ... HiFi Steakburgers ... Bank of America ... Armijo High School ... George's House of Liquor ... WOW Discount Market ...

United States Air Force
Travis A.F. Base

... Attention Visitors ... Assist Us in Assisting You ... Please Present Proper Identification ... Headquarters 22d Air Force ... Military Airlift Command ... Pride in Professional Performance ... An Equal Opportunity Employer ....

Evening, Sir. Go straight ahead to the stop sign after the next light, turn right, and go all the way to the end of the road. That'll be the parking lot. You'll see a lotta people and the operations tower. That's it.

In the waiting room, one meets those selected to man the frontiers of freedom. Two white-haired colonels mumble in military officialeze near the row of phone booths. Clusters of soldiers, sailors, and airmen play cards on suitcases or just wander around: staring out at the flight line, waging and losing battles against the discomfort of military uniforms, leafing through a phonebook, chewing on a candy bar. Most of those assigned to this flight, Hotel Twenty-Nine, sit in those pale green or tomato soup-red fiberglass chairs that violate all laws of comfort and seem to grow in herds wherever air terminals are built. No parents come into the waiting area; only a handful of girl friends are there.

A long night of nothing to do, nowhere to go, begins. Conversations are born, then allowed to die. Faces and expressions are studied, then ignored as they take on the uniform look of resignation. Eyes bound around the clinic-like terminal, from plastic signs to stainless steel signs to plastic signs:

> . . . Passenger Processing . . . Men . . . Ladies . . .
> Terminal Base Exchange . . . Cafeteria . . . Men . . .
> Firehose . . . Ladies . . . Lost and Found Luggage
> . . . In-Flight Meals . . . Are You Shipping Your
> Car Overseas? . . . Flight Insurance . . . .

Men fight for sleep in the impossible chairs; in most cases the chairs win. Giant jets nose up from the darkness a few hundred yards away, roaring engines pushing the earth down, rattling windows, chairs, teeth, baggage lockers.

. . . Space Available Roster . . . U.S. Army Pacific Personnel Liaison Team . . . Warning: 1. It Is a Crime to: A. Carry Concealed Weapons Aboard Aircraft, B. Interfere with Flight Crews, Including Any Steward or Stewardess, C. Transport Explosives, D. Seize an Aircraft . . . .

Your attention in the terminal, please. Attention in the terminal, please . . . will all passengers manifested on Continental Airlines government contract flight Yankee One Zulu Five for Anchorage, Alaska, and Honolulu, Hawaii, please check the name on their boarding pass . . . Mrs. Shrieber has lost her boarding pass. That is, Mrs. Shrieber has lost her boarding pass . . . .

. . . Things Go Better with Coke . . . No Admittance . . . Foreign Student Liaison . . . Army/Air Force VIP Lounge . . . Gate 2 . . . Entry for the Following Passenger Categories . . . No Visitors/Spectators Beyond This Point . . . .

Eight hours ago the sun slid down behind the venetian blinds. Now that same sun creeps back in through loading gate door frames and passenger entrances. B-52 bombers walk up onto the flight line and plow through the new day's heat waves, up and up to assume their Strategic Air Command vigil for a few hours.

. . . Coffee . . . cement-filled roll on a formica table . . . cold water shave . . . .

And then the long-awaited liberation:

May I have your attention in the terminal, your attention in the terminal, please. Travis Air Force Base announces the immediate departure of World Airways government contract flight Hotel Twenty-Nine for Da Nang, Vietnam, via Anchorage, Alaska, Atsugi, Japan, and Kadena Air Force Base, Okinawa. Passengers will board the aircraft through gate four in the following manner: all officers and civilians of equivalent rank, followed by all staff NCOs, followed by other enlisted personnel. You are reminded to retain one copy of your orders on your person at all times. Please extinguish all cigarettes at this time. No photographs are permitted on the flight line. Thank you.

All get up, join the somnolent hassle for a place in the hierarchy of the line, all except one very young soldier who wears the look of never having been farther away from home than boot camp. A girl clings to his left arm, dropping tears on his khaki shoulder. His is the only girl who stayed the night on those maddening chairs, stayed to be near him. He fights a trembling lip and growing embarrassment. Both are afraid he'll be killed, of course; but they can't know yet how good the chances are that he'll return. Next year they'll have to get to know each other all over again, and that might prove more painful than adjusting to death. He might not want to forget that warm girl he will meet on his R & R in Hong Kong or Tokyo, the girl who will make him feel like a man and beg him to take her with him to the States.

Hi, fellas, where you going?
Boo . . . Hiss . . . Oh, wow! Look at the set on her . . . Jesus Christ, lady . . . .

I'd like to introduce the crew and staff to you now. Our pilot today is Captain Thomas, the co-pilot is Lieutenant Rosen — he's the one with the curls, guys! And your flight engineer is Captain James. Please keep your seats as I introduce the girls now. Ha, ha, you're so cute, Colonel. Way in . . . .

Pinch her on the ass, Colonel . . . Fuck the lifers!

. . . the back is Carol, from Detroit. A little farther up is Dianne, from New Orleans. Behind me here is Suzie. She used to work at the Playboy Club in San Francisco — how about that one, men! In the galley is Janie, from Kansas City; and I'm Shirley from beautiful downtown Burbank — no guys, actually I'm from Los Angeles. If there is anything at all we can do for you, just let us know. Well, almost anything! Come on now, be nice. Oh, you're all so sweet, you sure don't look like killers! Now, Dianne and I will demonstrate the life jacket you'll find over each of your seats. If there's a chance we'll have to ditch over water, just reach straight above . . . .

Here we go to hell, escorted by the tight-hipped, Mabellined, hard-smiling, round-eyed stews from Never-Never Land. There's not much you can say about sixteen hours in a 707. It's just there and has to be endured. There's an exhilaration at takeoff despite the night before, and, what the hell, you're still 10,000 miles from it!

Above the clouds, excited conversation at many locations in the cabin gradually gives way to a general quiet. It is the quiet born of a train of mutual comprehensions — of female bodies under airline uniform camouflage, of the meaning of one's first foreign country, of the resemblance of clouds to known forms. There is an advancing numbness, first fought and then allowed supremacy in certain areas — the first to lose is your ass. One long and two short articles in a *Time* magazine after the first in-flight meal and:

Gentlemen, may I have your attention please. This is Captain Thomas speaking. Our flight plan has been changed since our departure from Travis. We will not be going to Anchorage, Alaska, but will go directly to Atsugi, Japan. I'll be keeping you posted on any further developments as they might occur.

By the time the second meal is consumed, all stewardesses have lost the capacity for bouncy comment and automated smiling. Service is now by the comatose, and the trivial again receives undue study:

... Life Vest Under Seat ... Gilet de Sauvetage Sous Seige ... No Smoking ... Defense de Fumer ... Fasten Seat Belt ....

Four meals, two magazines, and three naps later, Captain Thomas arrives with the cavalry to break the ordeal:

Gentlemen, we'll be landing at Atsugi very shortly. If you will look out the left side of the aircraft as we move into our landing pattern, you can see the snow-capped Mount Fuji through the clouds. We will have about a two-hour layover before going on to Okinawa. You will be allowed off the aircraft but you are restricted to the passenger terminal area. Your stewardess will give you further instructions.

In long lines at urinals and snack bars, the attrition rate on Hotel Twenty-Nine is obvious. It will be days before 165 metabolic rates recover from the assault of the International Dateline. A cold face-wash, a Coke, and aching positions are resumed.

Gentlemen, please fasten your seat belts as soon as you've taken your seats. Only a couple more hours and you'll be on dry, solid ground for a few days.

Instructions, seat belts, lift-offs, had taken on the familiarity and naturalness of body functions these last few hours or days or whatever.

Looks like this is your first tour in the Nam?
Yeah. My first tour. Hope it's not as bad as this damn flight.
This is a lot better than when I went the first time. We was on a ship out of San Diego. Took twenty-two days, and most of us were sick the whole time but about two days. This is the only way to go over, believe me! I just think about that first steam bath I'm going to get on Oki.
Gentlemen, we'll be touching down at Kadena Air Force Base in

24

*about ten minutes . . . please put out all cigarettes and fasten your
seat belts, please . . . the local time is eleven in the morning on the
fourth . . . the ground temperature is eighty-five degrees with clear
skies . . . .*

Okinawa. So this is Okinawa. The last battle of the big war. Here. Sake,
kamikazes, samurai swords, harakiri — the whole show. Right here. Khaki
forms file past painted stewardesses into an environment holding new possibilities for discomfort. A glaring sun forces eyelids into a tight squint;
JP-4 fumes flare out noses and lungs; and humidity clamps over every
pore. Western bodies — black and white, young and old — recoil from the
latest assault of the endless day.

Civilian 707s in bright colors — World Airways, Continental, TWA,
National — sit in a cluster near the control tower. A little farther out is a
perimeter of squat C-130s — the slow, droning birds with black bulbous
noses and squint-eyed windows — some silver, some in tan and dark brown
camouflage patterns. Next to the C-130s rest a pack of sleek, screaming
fighter bombers and that most beautiful and awesome piece of military
technology, the Phantom. At the farthest reaches of the flight line, segre-
gated from the others, the lord of the strip, the B52, relaxes between
missions.

It is difficult to get lost in this airport. There are only two kinds of people here, those on the way home and those on the way to Vietnam. In
addition to a different uniform, those home-bound wear the victor's gait
and a look of obvious relief. The new guys stand awkward, silent, self-
conscious, suddenly feeling a little immature, uninitiated, and wonder
what kind of an experience could cause an appearance so apparent on
those across the waiting room.

Men are always somewhat short of maturity until they have tasted the
deep uncertainty bred only by combat. And though they may still be less
than mature after seeing war, they will thereafter need no such base experience to erase that deficiency. On Okinawa, the mature and the incomplete were passing each other going in opposite directions. Here in the
humid air was a dichotomy: absolute confidence resting beside absolute
uncertainty. Half were "going south," as they would learn to say in the
next few days; they were not at all sure they would survive the experience. The other half, since they had already been there, were certain of

25

their survival; they were headed for the fantasyland of the Big PX, the *World*, Man — Stateside!

Find a seat on the first three buses, gentlemen.

Four short round-faced men begin to move four green army buses out of a parking lot that looks like any airport parking lot of any middle-sized American city. The only difference is the humid air.

Hey, what's that, Gunner?
That's a turtle-back tomb. They don't build them much any more, just the older people now. Japs used them for machine gun positions. Lotta my buddies got zapped from them back in forty-five, lot of them.
    ...Welcome to Camp Sukiran...United States Army, The Ryukus...Bolt Sell Store...Koza City...Honeymoon Hotel....

In Koza City, the green caravan with faces pressed to windows provokes a cheer from the group of GIs on liberty.

Keep your head and ass close to the deck, Sweetheart — Ha!
    ...Chibana...Asahi Beer...Bar Mary...Steam Bath and Cocktail Laungh Special Everything...Club Tennessee...Come see...We Have Special State-side Nudie Show from Australia... Ishikawa....
Look at that, a damn horse and wagon!
    ...Jewely Beuty Shop...Special Japan Bed Floor Look Show Every Night...Yaka Beach R & R Center...Little Tailor Special-ize For Custom Shirt...Combat Range 6...Kin Sanitarium... Camp Hansen....
Come right in, gentlemen. Move toward the front. Take the seats toward the front. Please, move it on up...Gentlemen, you should find on your desk two sheets of white paper stapled together, a blue card, and a white card. Please fill out the top half of the blue and white cards at this time — only the top half, gentlemen; do not write below the dotted line. Please follow directions; we don't want to keep you here any longer than necessary. Gentlemen, when you've

finished filling out your card, please pass it toward the center aisle. Keep the blue cards separate from the white; blue cards in this pile, Lieutenant. Gentlemen, as your papers are being endorsed, I want you to read this form very carefully. Then, when you're finished, I'll have some final word to pass before we get you out of here. We have more people who get delayed or into trouble because they can't follow these simple directions. Gentlemen, I call your attention to item seven. You must store all uniforms except the set you'll wear on the flight south in Building Twenty-six Fifty-four. All you'll have with you when you go is the uniform you'll wear, one set of civilian clothes for R & R, and your orders. That's all. Don't try to take all kinds of crap. Store it here, gentlemen, it's free. Your flight can store uniforms Friday morning from zero-nine to fifteen hundred. Do I have any questions? Good. Now some final word. Gentlemen, you are tentatively on Flight Hotel Twenty-Nine leaving the eighth, but check it when you sign in at the desk across the street in Building Twenty-six Thirty-six each day at ten hundred and at sixteen-thirty. E-six and above have all night liberty; E-four and E-five, until zero-two hundred; and E-three and below until midnight. E-five and below must have a liberty card. Civilian attire is authorized for all grades.

Tomorrow between zero-nine and twelve hundred, all of you will report to sickbay to have your shot cards checked. Don't lose the goddam thing. E-four and above may draw pay in advance not to exceed fifty dollars. Disbursing is in Building Twenty-six Nineteen. Day after tomorrow, all E-six and above will report to G-three, Building Twenty-two Fifty-one, for a tactical briefing, with documents proving you have a secret clearance. If anybody gets in trouble in town some night, we have MPs and a brig here, too, just like back in the World. And I would remind you that the VD rate on Oki is currently at ninety-seven percent. Good evening, gentlemen.

All the new arrivals on Oki wonder what their first veterans will look like, the ones who've been there. Like high school athletes curious about adversaries in a tentative way, they wonder how they will measure up next to the blooded. "They call them grunts, you know, the guys from the bush in Nam, and they're supposed to be the gungiest mothers around.

You can't miss 'em." Do they stick out because they have more starch in their uniforms, or less? Are they bigger, do they look older? The first ones seen are remembered. They amble out of the barracks at about nine in the morning and take a direct route across the grass (in violation of Base Order 4010.2b) to the snack bar in the bowling alley, then on to the PX, with its stereo corner, its magazine rack. Watching them you see why they don't need to wear medals or bandages to make it known where they've been the past year. Once-black boots have turned white from the sun and paddies. The cover rests on the back of a thick wad of hair, and out from under it creep the beginnings of sideburns to challenge more regulations. Hair rests on the back of the collar, hair keeps the nose and lower lip spaced properly. Hair, hair — it pisses off the lifers! The saluting hand is in a pocket, the other flips a lighter top open and shut. The eyes — no thousand-yard stares here. Instead, an intense darting that bores through to an evaluation in seconds. And the walk, an exclusive and temporal possession from the experience. They will lose it some day, as Vietnam recedes into two years, five, ten. They don't quite swagger or strut, but they are beyond conforming to anyone's cadence but their own. It comes from two things: months of trying to move one's body and about thirty-five or seventy pounds through paddies and over hills while using as little energy as possible, and the final jubilation of each nerve and muscle cell in the realization that it's all over at last — they'll never have to carry that fucking pack or radio again. Move into their path and pick up the vocabulary, the interests . . .

> an' it surprised me too, ya know, gettin' tight with a gunny but he was all right . . . helped me get the R&R I wanted . . . She still writes me, too — you seen her pitcher yet? . . . If I can draw some advance pay this afternoon I'm gonna get me them speakers we was lookin' at yesterday, the Panasonics, you know . . . hey, you remember that guy used to try and make it to sickbay every day we had a hike on Parris Island? The son of a bitch got a Silver Star on that Operation Liberty Two! A guy out in the vill told me last night — he was with him when he did it . . . .

But the picture is still incomplete. One discovers, as the result of tired and aimless wandering about the camp, the place where the young veterans let it all hang out. Building 2412 is the base library, and it is one of the very few comfortable buildings available to the junior enlisted man both day and night. Its popularity rests on one characteristic.

Hey, Man, where we goin' today?
Got any jing?
I told you. They fucked up my pay record in Nam.
Well, I got some, but not enough for the vill again. We'll go to the library.
To the what? Who in the fuck you trying to jack anyway?
A guy told me in the mess hall today — it's fucking air-conditioned. Open till ten every night. And it ain't just for the heavies. It's for everybody, and it's free!
Air-conditioned? You mean slope air conditioning, or Stateside air conditioning?
They got real Stateside machines in there, Tripper, the real motors.

The troops make no pretense of scholarly pursuit. Here they come to be by themselves, to crawl into themselves, to inch cautiously back to the thought patterns of a peaceful, pleasurable existence. Here they have none of the attitudinal adornments displayed in the presence of civilians. In the morning, they come in, head straight for the reading tables, the stacks, and just crash — sleep — until Okinawa cools off. Places nearest the air conditioning ducts go first, then the cushioned chairs and couches, then the floor spaces in between. Nothing but wall-to-wall green marines, crashed out in beautiful dreams. Very rarely does one snore. It's as if they want to be in the deepest possible state of relaxation while maintaining just enough consciousness to preserve an awareness of the cool luxury in the air. Nor is the stereo room off-limits. Some stay all day, plugged into the soul sounds, the country and western, the acid rock or the "Golden Oldies" — eyes closed, lips forming the words of peace and love, heads bobbing to a new beat, absorbed inward in dreams of the cars they'll buy at home, the girls they'll chase and win, the homecoming parties without end . . . .

I been sweating for a year, Man. In here you don't even sweat! It's outa sight, Man, fucking outa sight!

29

Though they were still 1,400 miles from the war farther south, young Americans on the way to it got an introduction to some of its direct effects at places like Kin Village and Koza City on Okinawa. During the 1960s the term "camp follower" implied a greater variety of activities and businesses than ever before, but central to it all was still the timeless theme of lonely boy far from home meets pretty girl. In places like Kin and Koza, soldiers and marines found girls refreshingly uninhibited but maddening and depressing in their relentless drive for the American dollar. If anyone ever invents a machine to do nothing but separate a human being from his legal tender, surely it will resemble the town across from the main gate of any military base the world over. In any one of the hundreds of bars, the story is the same.

Well, hello, and what's your name?

Me, Sachiko, wha's you name?

You can call me Bob, I'm from Denver — how 'bout you, Sachiko?

I from Henoko — that way — this you firs' time Okinawa, Bob-a-san?

Ha! Bob-a-san — ja hear that D. J.?

Yeah, this is my first time in Okinawa. I think I like Oki very much. How 'bout you showing me around the island some time?

Sure, I show you. Say, you want drinky now, Bob-a-san?

Yeah, I'll have a beer, Sachiko, an' get whatever you want, too.

Campai. Bob-a-san . . . hey, Bob-a-san, you like me? Maybe we hab many drinky, hab good time tonight — maybe pray honeymoon rater, eh?

Yeah, sounds good, Sachiko. Yeah, I like you jus' fine.

Let's go, Pal, we can do better than this.

Soon, over and over:

Hey, you big han'some GI, maybe we go pray honeymoon apter tweb 'crock, eh?

Well, how did you do last night, Pal? I lost you after the Napoleon Club.

Oh, Man, she was something else. "I show you number one Japanese way tonight," she said. I gotta find her again!

30

Hey, you hear about George? Dropped a hundred-thirty last night, on the same broad, and all he got outa the deal was a steam bath. She wouldn't go honeymoon with him. He'll probably do it again, though. He's definitely got no brains and a lotta bread.

Days and nights turn into a barhopping routine having damn little variety and less logic. Out of money, the uneasiness about the future becomes sharper to the privates first class and the lance corporals. They kill time wandering around the base, looking over stereos and tape decks in the PX, or lying in the heat of the barracks studying the intricacies of springs under mattresses overhead. Okinawa is not the end of this trip. Their time too drawing near, the new lieutenants retreat to the Officers' Club to wrestle with facts and thoughts getting heavier each day.

What the hell, I didn't come over here to screw every slant-eyed broad I could find.

Over seven-sevens and whiskey sours they remind each other in silence where they're going, that many other lives will soon depend on their abilities to read a map, reach a quick decision.

What if I screw up?

Each little fragment of doctrine thrown at them in the last seven months becomes the most important class they ever received, just like the instructors used to say;

Maybe they shoulda given us a class on how to write letters of condolence?
Hey, ferget it, Man, here have another one . . . .

Finally, long after the you-buy-me-drinky-we-play-honeymoon swindle has lost all novelty, troop handlers walk briskly through barracks buildings around the sickbay and base headquarters.

Fall out! Hey, git that guy outa the rack there, Hotel Twenty-Nine on the road!

31

It is an order eagerly followed. The young warriors-to-be move quickly through the heat. Ranks form, bodies are counted, buses are boarded. And 500 yards away at the "O" Club on the coral mound:

May I have your attention in the club, your attention please. All officers manifested on Hotel Twenty-Nine please muster at the main entrance to the club, that is . . . .

A few of the 165 have found a new girl these past six days. For them, there would be an additional source of mail during the next year, but now on the buses back to Kadena, most thoughts were 1,400 miles beyond Camp Hansen or the "Lucky Hearts Club." Of the journey to war by jet, only three hours remained.

Welcome back, men! Aw, come on, don't look so glum — we'll all be back together again next year. At this time I'd like to introduce . . . our flying time will be two hours forty-three minutes . . . we will serve beverages during the flight but no meal . . . will demonstrate the life preservers to be found . . . . Good afternoon, gentlemen, this is your captain speaking. This afternoon we'll be flying at an altitude of approximately twenty-two thousand feet . . . we expect excellent weather all the way . . . .

No one slept this time. All were quiet and alert, none betraying his last revel in the vill the night before. As time and distance ran out, a nervous anxiety was manifested. Finally, about an hour from the destination, soft voices broke the tense silence. The hard reality was upon all now; its terrible possibilities no longer seemed far-away, not-me things. Stewardesses were no longer stared at, though some worked hard at hearing an American female voice right up to the last minute. There were only two sailors on the entire plane. Both were very young and both were going to be medical corpsmen with the marines in the field. One began turning white as the big jet dropped into its landing pattern over Da Nang.

Ah, 'scuse me, Sir. Who you, ah, gonna be with when we get there?
I'm not sure yet. I could stay in Da Nang for awhile or go right out with a company as soon as I report in. How about yourself?

32

Well, my buddy here and I, we're both corpsmen and we'll be with some Marine unit somewhere — probably in the field . . . you, ah, know what it's like out there?

Well, I've never been there, of course, but it's not that bad — not as bad as the veterans in the bars tell it.

I sure hope so. But I heard a lotta corpsmen get it when they're helpin' guys that got hit — an' the VCs look to knock out the corpsman, the corpsman and the radioman.

Well, there's no sense worrying too much now. You've had good training, you'll do all right, Doc.

Yeah, it shouldn't be too bad, I'll be plenty busy . . . it shouldn't be too bad.

The men, the kids — joking, talking, staring — didn't seem so foolish in their vanities, their pretensions. They didn't know what was about to happen to them and they were a little happy in their ignorance. All were certain their lifestyle would be drastically changed; many, however, would soon be amazed when they realized how many of the safe, hometown routines could be preserved. But parents, of course, knew that every son was dodging bullets and pungi stakes every day — ". . . in the bush. That's what my kid Ronnie calls the front lines. Yeah, he's right up there, right up there! Got a letter just yesterday, says he saw his first dead body!"

Gentlemen, we'll be touching down in Da Nang, Vietnam in about ten minutes. The local time is now two in the afternoon on the twelfth, and the ground temperature is ninety-six degrees with a clear sky. Please extinguish all cigarettes and fasten your seat belts, please. On behalf of the entire crew and staff, I'd like to say we've enjoyed having you with us on World Airways government contract flight Hotel Twenty-Nine, and we hope to see all of you again next year on your way home. Good-bye and good luck.

33

2

Bravo One-Three

In a branch of the armed forces most conscious of its history and image before the public, 1st Battalion of the Third Marine Regiment is comparatively unknown outside its own ranks. Though consistently manned by a fair share of heroic individuals, the unit has rarely been a headline-maker. But while there was less glory, there is a history. After chasing Dominican rebels and Mexican bandits, One-Three sat out all of World War I and was disbanded in the early 1920s. Twenty years later it was reactivated and bore a major share of the fighting in the Bougainville and Guam campaigns of World War II. During the Korean War the battalion and the entire parent Third Marine Division cruised around the Far East, pulling liberty in Manila and Hong Kong, sailing around the Korean peninsula waiting for an emergency. General MacArthur never called. During the next twelve years the only casualties the battalion sustained were those from brawls in the bars and bordellos of various liberty ports in the Pacific.

Twelve years after the ceasefire in Korea there was a call. President Johnson landed American ground troops at Da Nang, Vietnam on the morning of March 8, 1965. The first ashore were from 3d Battalion 9th Marines and 1st Battalion 3d Marines. In the next four and one-half years, One-Three would see more action than in her previous thirty-four years.

On April 19, 1969, "B" Company, 1st Battalion, 3d Marines was taken off Operation Maine Crag after forty-five consecutive days in the field near the Laotian border, twenty-eight miles south of the Demilitarized Zone. Maine Crag had been embarrassingly fruitless for Bravo Company: only six North Vietnamese soldiers sighted and four killed in those forty-five days. Beyond that action there was nothing but too much boredom, exhaustion, thirst, immersion foot and jungle rot, the painful skin eruptions that fester and never heal in the bush.

During the first week in April the regimental commander had flown out to inspect the fire support base Bravo Company had just built. He was not impressed by the ragged, exhausted appearance of the troops and directed a three-day rehabilitation for the entire Company at the division's in-country R & R center. After a six-hour trip by helicopter, truck, and U.S. Navy river boat, the troops walked onto the white coastal sands at the mouth of the Cua Viet River on the South China Sea. They dropped packs and rifles, and learned to smile and laugh again in the cool surf, cold beer in one hand, steak in the other. And on their third afternoon on the beach, the troops got to see again what a real round-eye looked like when the Division Special Services Office scheduled a show with four real live Australian girls and a band.

> "Wow! Look at them knockers, and that long hair, and can you imagine what it'd be like having them long, long legs wrapped around you, and her working out for all she's worth? Jeez, Man, someday . . . ."

A rehab normally lasts only three days but this one had stretched to ten; plenty of time for the jungle rot to dry out and heal, even enough time to get a suntan. It was definitely over, though. A couple days before, people had begun to sense it in the air. Soon the mutual sensation became a freely-voiced rumor: "Oh, yes Sir, that's straight skinny right from the Colonel's radioman!" But there were really only two things to do until confirmation of the new "operation" came through: drink beer and crash on the beach.

"Operation" is probably the biggest misnomer of all. There is nothing antiseptic, nothing surgically precise about a search and destroy sweep, nothing predictable like some anatomical structure or disorder. They usually start on the designated "H-hour" as planned, but thereafter blunder on, in something closer to chaos than plan, to either a bloody climax or a quiet and uneventful conclusion. And there are days on which the worst enemies of an American field unit are exhaustion, stupidity, and the short-sightedness of its own leaders and troops.

In any event, every operation begins with an "Op Order," an officiously-worded document of some forty-two or seventy-seven or one hundred nine typed pages of intelligence estimates, logistics appendices, and tactical concepts. The best reading is usually found in the paragraph labeled "Mission." Here the general's wordsmiths go all out to inject the fighting spirit into the lower-echelon commanders: "1st Battalion (Reinforced) will, on order, occupy and defend designated objectives in the assigned Tactical Area of Responsibility, and thereafter, by the maximum use of supporting arms and aggressive patrolling techniques . . . ." Such blushing prose always provides a short respite from the boredom and nagging fear in war. "Make sure your troops run aggressive patrols now, not just them regular old SOP jobs—Ha!"

On the afternoon of April 27, 1969, the company commander and four platoon commanders of Bravo One-Three were sitting in their tent on the beach, drinking beer and looking over the newest operation order. Here was the final word, the dreaded confirmation of the dreaded rumor. It was to be called Operation Virginia Ridge and it would start at six in the morning the day after tomorrow. Participating units would be the 1st and 2d battalions of the 3d Marine Regiment and the 37th ARVN Ranger Battalion. "Well, at least they didn't name the damn op after the general's wife's parakeet."

"Yeah, looks like it's in a pretty good area, too . . . about twenty miles west of here . . . Be sure and tell your people to get rid of their beer tonight, we don't want to give any of it back."

Each man could feel this fat document burn a little in his hands as it was read, passed around, discussed. A whole new series of unexpected incidents would be faced in the next few weeks, and since war rarely duplicated its tangled challenges, past experience was not an infallible guide. New decisions with new consequences would have to be made. The responsibility for timely decisions and for life itself was underlined, renewed. But to other people this document meant other things.

Here in this op order was the unpublicized counter to the highly publicized *esprit de corps* of the United States Marine Corps. It was the ages-old animosity between front-line infantrymen and the staff and support personnel farther back — the "pogues," those "rear-echelon mother-fuckers!" Those who wrote the op orders never had to carry them out, never had to walk that little two and a half inches on the map that turned into a man-killing three thousand two hundred meters on the ground, the 3200 meters on a flat piece of colored paper on a flat table that grew into five thousand meters up hills and down streambeds. And no matter how hard they tried to send out the needed water and C-rations and mail and new socks, if it didn't get off the landing zone and out to the companies in the bush today, well that's okay, the rear pogues still got to sleep on their Stateside mattresses after seeing a movie every night or a live USO show twice a week. But that wasn't all they had back there in the rear. On top of all those bennies they had ice cream and ice-cold beer! Quite naturally the sentiment was: "Them turds in the rear ain't worth a flying fuck, not one of them! If they gotta put down their cold beer for five minutes to cut somebody a hus they won't do it. Shit-worthless pogues!"

Anyway, with this operation order printed and distributed, the staff horses' work was largely finished. Now it was time for the privates first class and the sergeants, the lieutenants and the corporals to take over, to conduct those "aggressive" patrols, to "seek out, close with and destroy the enemy by all available means," which means anything from a Phantom jet to a knuckle sandwich.

After ten days at Cua Viet, Bravo Company was in pretty good shape. Defective weapons, toothaches, broken eyeglasses, jungle rot, and empty stomachs had all been taken care of. And the troops were hung over. About the only remaining need was that for willing women, and there wasn't much anybody could do about that one, not even the general. There had been the boom-boom girls from Cua Viet Village hanging around the perimeter wire, but if anyone ever touched one it was a guaranteed case of the clap. So that craving had to be set aside until R & R or rotation back home. But no matter how suntanned and satisfied the grunts were now they would still have been in pretty fair shape as a combat unit without the rehab, for they had one advantage no NVA company could draw on. Bravo Company had Captain Gerald H. Samson.

In the vocabulary of the grunt there is one word that indicates an individual's worth in the bush, in war. If someone is "gungi," he's all right, it's good to have him on our side, he's afraid of nothing, he never gets tired, he can be counted on to help in any tight situation, and he's probably a little crazy. The gungi individual also likes to kill a little more than is necessary. Most of his troopers honestly believed that if the President would let him, Sam would take his Company into Hanoi, capture the city and take Ho Chi Minh prisoner. That's gungi.

There was no sense in even trying to describe anybody as being gungier than Captain Sam — the person just didn't exist. No one could hump faster, no one knew tactics better, no one had more discipline or deeper respect for the concept of duty, and not very many others liked to kill VC and NVA as much as Sam. There were even rumors that he had killed some prisoners a few months before in a manner less than humane, but what the hell, they were only rumors and they were only "gooks." The story only added confirmation to his reputation. He was paid as a captain, but all knew that Sam held the permanent rank of Gungi Mother Supreme.

Sam was a full-blooded Lumbe Indian, born in the small Indian town of Pembroke, North Carolina. The grunts accepted that as the reason he was so crazy, so quiet, so humorless. "Ah shit, you never can tell what them Indians are thinking." He had been in the Marine Corps fifteen years. It usually takes only thirty months to make the rank of captain, so fifteen years made Sam a "mustang," an enlisted man who was offered a commission because of his demonstrated leadership and military knowledge. Captain Sam was feared and hated, but he was also obeyed and followed. He was the kind of leader who could make the grunts do what they had to do to go home alive. For those who met, worked with, and left Sam in war, it was impossible to imagine him in any other environment. He seemed born to it and for it. War allowed him expression and he performed the master.

Bravo Company had someone else at the start of this new op too, but someone looked on as more a source of entertainment than an asset: a new second lieutenant. Carl Andrews turned out to be one of those faceless individuals of the population the military has a way of bringing out of the shadows and building into something at least a little useful.

Andrews had first come to the attention of the grunts because he was the newest arrival — a "newby" — which meant he couldn't really lead or command anyone without at least hearing some war stories from the PFCs and corporals, without asking the lower rankers, the ones who called themselves "us peons," what to do in this or that situation. But shortly after his arrival at Cua Viet, still before his name was known to all, Andrews was noted for another reason, one which marked him apart from other newby junior officers: not only did he not have to be here in the bush with Bravo, Andrews didn't even have to be in the Marines or any other component of the military.

Before he joined the Corps, Andrews had a completely safe job in the World. He was a teacher and as such, exempt from the draft. But, bored after two years and curious about what war was really like, he volunteered for the only one going at the time. Though many of them had done the same thing, the troops who later got word of Andrews' story found it incredible, and were not notably reluctant to tell him so. "You mean, Sir, you was a teacher in the World looking at all that young ass in them mini-skirts all day long, and you quit to join the Green Machine? Excuse me, Sir, but with all due respect, your mother raised a fool!"

One year after his enlistment Andrews was in Vietnam but with a rear-echelon unit as an administrative officer. Following a six month wait that seemed more like six years, he was walking across the white sandy beaches of Cua Viet, looking for the Bravo Company post.

"Bravo? Yeah, they're over that way, second row, fourth tent. You'll see the guidon stuck in the sand."

Andrews found the company pennant, walked up to the tent behind it and parted the entrance flap. He saw eight men sitting on cots and heard one voice. Captain Samson was lying on his back, a shaving mirror propped on the dark green undershirt covering his chest. He squinted into the glass, thrust his jaw forward, twisted his mouth off to one side and with a pair of huge scissors cut away the hairs that contributed nothing to the striking appearance of his mustache. While he did that he talked out of the free corner of his mouth.

"I distinctly remember telling you people last night I wanted all the ammo policed up and put in boxes and labeled by platoons and squads, and then put it all in an empty tent down across from third platoon. Then I go out and check it this morning and I find out it ain't been done. And I find a squad leader who says he never even heard nothing about policing up no ammo and his squad's all out swimming so it'd be a couple of hours before he could get it done. Now I thought I made it clear it's important we get that ammo all collected in one place under guard so we don't have nobody getting killed by no accidental discharges while they're supposed to be relaxing here, and we don't have nobody getting fragged, and none of that race riot shit."

The Captain was not screaming. His voice was very low-pitched, slow-paced, sonorous. It was a voice more appropriate to tired and bored travelers discussing the weather in a small-town bus terminal. One could almost fall asleep listening to it. But that wasn't quite right really, for Andrews noticed that when this man behind the dark complexion and the laser-beam eyes spoke, the other seven men listened. And most of these men in the tent were large men, men of proven strength and leadership ability. Before today he had expected rifle company commanders to have profane, booming voices. Another misconception brought from the World.

"Now that's the kind of shit, gentlemen, that don't get it in this here Company. When I pass the word and every one of you there says you understand, I expect things to get expedited, and right. Now if you can't expedite things around here like they should, just let me know and I'll tell the Colonel and we'll have somebody else out here doing it right and you can go on back to the rear with the pogues in the club. If that's the way you want it, that is."

The new lieutenant heard that voice two more times on his first day with the Company. The next time was in the late afternoon, just before a pair of leggy and busty Australians teased the troops with mini-skirts, a few kisses, and songs about home at the weekly USO show on the beach. It was a briefing by the Captain on the Company and the character of the platoon Andrews would be assigned to lead. It was all part of Sam's show for newbys and it came off beautifully. He was glad to get another volunteer for the bush but he couldn't show any warmth or humor, couldn't give any indication that the next few months would resemble anything pleasant. The exterior had to be cold and hard to insure that these soft-skinned college kids they were giving commissions to nowadays wouldn't

41

get too uppity in the near future. "Understand you been in the rear for awhile."

"Yessir. Everyone got a platoon as soon as we got over except me."

"You out here cuz you want to be?"

"Oh yes, Sir, I really do want it."

"Well, that's okay but don't look for any skating job out here — we're all pretty tight cuz we have to be. Okay, you're going to third platoon. Get to know your platoon sergeant and squad leaders these next few days, and you can learn a lot from these PFCs we got here too, but don't let them get the idea they're running that show there. Some of them get pretty damn salty after they been here a few months. You got a lot to unlearn and a lot to learn. And I know the crazy fucking ideas some of you hot-shots come over here with but you can forget about pulling any crazy crap just to get the big medal. Don't look for any free Bronze and Silver Stars — there's none of that end-of-tour shit here as long as I got this Company. We got more than our share of medals here. You talk around to some of the troops and you'll find every one of them was earned. Okay, go on over to your platoon now. Third tent over."

The last time Andrews heard the voice on that first day with Bravo was that night in the staff and officers' tent. The beer had been flowing freely and Captain Samson was holding forth on one of his favorite topics, the inevitability of the next war. "What do you mean 'if' there's another war? Shit, you know there's gonna be one — just look at history. It averages out to every fifteen years there's a war. And just look at these so-called 'statesmen' we got now. Shit — Russians telling us to get screwed, us telling China to get screwed, all these petty-ass dictators in these new countries always fighting and trying to buy up our planes and tanks and ships, and look at the Arabs and Jews. There's gotta be another war. Just look at history — every fifteen years!" This first day with Captain Sam and Bravo One-Three would be one of those in his life Andrews would never have any trouble remembering.

In the early afternoon of April 29, Captain Sam put his Company back on the Navy river launch and started back up the Cua Viet River to Dong Ha. There the Company boarded trucks and were taken down Route Nine. They spent the night in an open grassy field seventeen miles west of Dong Ha and two miles east of the artillery base at the Rockpile.

Bravo was up and on the move by five the next morning; one hundred forty-seven Americans were moving, in most cases reluctantly, back to the reality of being grunts. The life of a grunt in Vietnam was not noteworthy for its variety of experience. There was heat, thirst, walking, boredom, fear, blood and death; a succession of events only rarely broken by things pleasant — beer and letters. One part of that reality would, in the next few days, be much more conspicuous than the others — the humping over hills and through all kinds of vegetation with anywhere from thirty-five to seventy pounds on one's back.

This first day's hump was to be of moderate length, 6000 meters, or six "clicks," and there was a road most of the way so it should have been easy, a skate. But since it was Bravo's first hump after 108 cases of beer, 750 steaks, and ten days of slack during the rehab on the coast, it turned out to be an "ass-kicker." The Company had to stop twice and send its corpsmen up and down the column to pop the pills — give out salt tablets. By eleven they were at the objective, Fire Support Base Pete. The rehab and the bennies were all sweated and vomited out now, parts of the irretrievable past. FSB Pete had been occupied and abandoned by another unit about a month before, so all that had to be done to prepare the defenses of the hill was clean the C-ration cans and other junk out of the incoming holes on the perimeter. Digging into the earth of Vietnam was rarely this easy.

At one in the afternoon the maddening reality that was the "combat situation in Eye Corps Tactical Zone" began to make itself felt on the grunts of Bravo One-Three when Captain Sam called his platoon commanders up to the top of Pete. "Battalion just called up and changed the word. We gotta move again today. We got three choppers coming in a half hour so break your people down into heli-teams and have them standing by all packed and ready to go. We'll be lifted about eight or nine clicks, then we link up with the ARVN and Two-Three and hump a couple clicks before we set in for the night. I'll call you back when the birds are on the way. Yeah, I thought we was gonna stay here for awhile too, but they say this here stop was just to get us in position for the start of the op."

So the lieutenants went back and told the sergeants, who bitched about the word change, and the sergeants went back and told the corporals, who bitched about the word change, and the corporals went down to the foxholes and told the privates and lance corporals, who bitched about the word change, and then everybody packed up and sat down in the holes and grass around the landing zone to wait for the choppers and bitch some more about the word change. After the word change had circulated around the hill, another circulated in its wake. It was the common reaction among marines to all abrupt direction changes: "Eat the apple, fuck the Corps."

This would be Bravo's first heli-lift in over four months. That fact alone should have provoked some optimism, maybe even a little excitement — the heavies and pogues in the rear were actually doing something to help the grunts out of a nine-click hump, and maybe things would be different from now on, maybe there wouldn't be so much senseless walking all the time and everywhere. Maybe the Corps would start heli-lifting the grunts everywhere — like the Army. "Them Army guys know how to do it — they ride whenever they go someplace — none of this humping shit!" But these were marines on FSB Pete and so they brought the marines' cynicism to the situation: "Don't hold your breath waiting for that, they'll find some way to fuck us over. Just watch."

After the morning's move the rest of the day could hardly be viewed with anything akin to optimism. In the morning the grunts had been reminded what a dull, hot, one-step-at-a-time thing an operation was. Waiting faces showed the deep resignation of "goddam, here we go again — back to the same old shit!" There would have to be at least this one more op before R & R, before rotation back to the World, before — Ha! — the war would end. No one was actually tired from the morning hump, but no unnecessary moves were being made while waiting around the landing zone. Packs are always heavy at the start of an op, and strength would be needed for the afternoon. The hills get steeper farther west and that's where Virginia Ridge was. The squinting grunts sat down and leaned on each other back-to-back, staring off into the green and blue hills, the hills beginning to quiver in the early afternoon heat. Conversation was stripped to the minimum, but there was still room for the black humor produced by every generation going to war: "You know, Lieutenant, if I get wounded on this one it'll be bad enough, you know, Ma crying and the whole bad scene. But if I get killed I'll really be pissed!" And on the other side of the LZ:

"Nine times, I had it nine times," says one grinning trooper.

"Bull."

"Yeah, you talk to the corpsman, he's got my book. It's all there, clap, nine times!"

44

The quiet ones were the newbys. They studied the veterans, strained to catch every comment, eager to see what they should be doing now, what they should seem to be thinking on the eve of this big First Time in the Bush Against the Enemy. They were a little elated over the prospect of being soon baptized in fire, but what they heard was not quite what they had expected men on the eve of battle would be saying. "I know I'm gonna get it, Man, it's just a matter of time, you know? But just before it happens I'd like to have that Raquel Welch drop her pants and sit square on my face — just once, Man, just once."

And elsewhere, "You know, Behl, I swear you stink more every day I know you."

"That ain't me, that's my ear."

"Your ear? What do you mean your ear?"

"That's the ear I got off the first gook I killed back on Taylor Common, down south."

"You mean you been carrying that fucking thing since Taylor Common, four months ago? What the hell you trying to prove?"

"Fucking A I still carry it. I ain't trying to prove nothing. I just like it. He was my first gook. I got a picture of his girl, too."

"You're fucking sick, Behl. The Nam's getting to you. And don't expect me to share no foxhole with you long as you keep that rotten ear. You're sick, Behl."

"You think I'm sick, huh? You wait'll you been here eight and a half months. You just wait."

At still another place on the hill, Gunnery Sergeant Herman Randall broke the hot silence surrounding the new and pensive Lieutenant Andrews. "Yeah, Lieutenant, don't worry about that round with your name on it. There's nothing you can do about that one. Just watch out for all those ones marked 'To whom it may concern!' "

Soon three black specks could be made out against the clear blue sky; the telltale whump-whump sound followed. Faces lifted to the west to judge how much longer they could remain seated in their patch of shade. The old familiar rubbery feeling, as before the big game — how many seasons ago? — came to legs and shoulders, senses sharpened. Here and there troops gulped down the last of a can of peaches or pineapple chunks, issued a few "oh shits" to no one in particular, and put on their helmets. The choppers moved into descending circles; the whump-whump became clearer, loud, deafening. One at a time they touched down and lowered their ramps.

Fifteen troops grabbed the pack of the man in front, leaned forward and fought through the stinging tornado of dust and rocks raised by the bird's twin rotors. They kneeled inside the cigar-shaped fuselage, holding onto cargo netting and each other as the bird lifted and leaned to the northeast. Up 500, 1000, 2000 feet and one's outlook on the world and the war underwent a dramatic improvement: the heat was gone. This beautiful, beloved, vibrating chopper had lifted the grunts away from the heat. They looked at each other, gazed out the windows and side-hatches, closed their eyes and smiled as the cool gusts whipped through the chopper's insides, down under pack straps and flak jackets, up pant legs into crotches and armpits and ears. "Shit, this Vietnam place ain't so bad. I could probably hump six, eight more clicks today."

From a time of gnawing thirst and anger at a change in plans, the grunts had been moved into a time and place of something near ecstasy by this beautiful green helicopter. But the grunts were now having one of the larger, more cruel jokes of life and war played on them. Soon the chopper would drop back down into the green and the heat, and they would see how life in the bush could be spectacular one day, stupifying the next. For the next four days it would be mostly the latter. In another day, the rehab at Cua Viet would seem a year-ago thing; in two days it would be a decade ago; in four days it would seem so far in the past there would be little sense in even saying it ever happened.

The choppers circled, one began to fall away from the others and the grunts came alive, got ready to jump off the ramp and run. When the bird was still a few hundred feet over the landing zone the grunts' senses were raised to another level of acuity by a sharp sound, familiar but unwelcome, cutting through the whump-whump and rattle of the big green bird. It was the sharp crack and whine of American and North Vietnamese rifles assaulting each other, answering each other. There was nothing superfluous in the deadly, metallic conversation. There was a second of silence, then a burst of a dozen shots, signifying that helmets and uniforms had been discerned from the green of everything, then an answering burst from the discovered, and the cycle repeated itself. Fear and anxiety ended the coolness of the heli-lift.

The birds dropped fast, jamming stomachs up into lungs, banged down

46

on the lip of a thousand pound bomb crater. The grunts stumbled out, leaned away from the filthy prop-wash and lunged for the nearest green they could find. They felt much too exposed, naked. But as the chopper lifted away, taking its screeching and whumping sound up and back to the southwest, the crack and whine seemed farther away. Too far away to push one flat against the earth.

"Anybody know who's catching it over there?"

"The Lieutenant says it's the ARVN got some NVA trapped over that next ridge."

"Get some, ARVN, get some so we won't have to do it tomorrow, baby."

The birds came back again and again, dropped the rest of the grunts on the bomb crater, lifted and headed back home. At two in the afternoon of April 30, Bravo Company was in position to begin assaulting the string of objectives. The operation was no longer the generals' or the colonels'. It now belonged to the captains and corporals, the PFCs and lieutenants. Virginia Ridge was heating up.

It was easy going at first. There was a long downhill slope and then a stream, which meant a cooling dip and a long drink, authorized or not, before starting up the other side. Most important for the moment, the grunts could see where they were going.

"You mean it's that hill over there, the bald mother?"

"Yeah, the Lieutenant says that's the one. Hell, this ain't been a bad day. Now if them gooks just don't chase them NVA up there tonight we'll be okay."

These were the things that made thirteen months in the Nam bearable — a stream and a drink just ahead, the objective within sight and maybe only a click away, a letter on the way from the girl, R & R only a month away, the bennies strung out along the way, breaking up thirteen months into chunks of weeks and days.

"Yeah, this is going okay. Kind of pretty scenery, too. No 'Get Right With God' or 'See Rock City' signs around here either."

The one hundred forty-seven grunts of Bravo inched down off the first slope of the afternoon in single file, down toward the flat grassy plain with its refreshing wet "blue line" in the middle. As the lead elements reached it, Sam came in on the radio.

"This is Six! Tell your people they can stop at this here blue line, but to fill only two canteens, then move on across, expedite that thing down there. We gotta get up this here objective quick."

So they stopped, scooped helmetsful of the warm brown water over their heads, gulped handsful, filled canteens, and moved on and up. Now a pair of choppers appeared overhead, both small "hueys," not the troop carriers. One swooped in low over the stream area in a back-and-forth pattern, north to south, east to west. The second stayed up higher. It was the Battalion Commander and the Commander of the 37th ARVN Rangers, the unit supposedly doing the firing half an hour before. The heavies didn't come out to offer anybody another rehab. They came to make sure the operation got off to the best possible start.

"This is Six! That's the big man up there and he says he sees too many people bunched up down around that blue line. Get them spread out and down outa sight when they're not moving."

The column inched on up the hill. The remaining grunts were thinned out around the stream but the man in the circling bird still wasn't satisfied.

"This is Six! The big man is still seeing a cluster-screw. I told you to expedite that thing down there. Now get them damn people up off their asses and either moving or spread out. I better not hear any more today about any bunching up!"

Now the Colonel had aroused Sam, touched close to his pride in himself, his pride that his Bravo Company was not just another bunch of ground-pounders who had no discipline, who would bunch it up and just shoot the shit when there was a hump to complete through enemy territory, a firefight to find, a war to be won. Sam was bitching and the heat was rising; it might not turn out to be such a good day after all.

It took an hour to get everybody up that hill. It had been "prepped," prepared by bombardment, an hour before by Navy jets, so there was no tangled vegetation, no "wait-a-minute" vines to hack through with a dull machete, but the air was still heavy with the nauseous fumes of napalm. The only opposition was from the heat, the grade of the slope, and the weight of a pack and ammunition belt. No NVA today. During that hour the heat started to get to Bravo. There were three heat casualties — three dizzy, flushed and dry bodies with arm and leg muscles twitching. One of the three was Gunny Randall. He made an impression on the troops who saw him lying there panting in short gasps much more lasting than that made by his 260 pounds in the dirt of the hillside. Gunny was not "short in the Nam" but he was definitely "short in the machine," having only nineteen more months to go before his twenty-year career as a marine was completed. Then he would go back home to Maine where, as he did not hesitate to tell it, "I'll have my hands full — a fishing pole in my left and my right hand taking that retirement check from the mailman." All the grunts knew he had seen a lot of shit in Korea; they figured anybody who had done almost eighteen years on active duty and had walked out of the Chosin Reservoir — "frozen Chosin" — could take a breather now and then. "How about a swig or a piece of gum, Gunny?" On top at last, the grunts could look down to see the hill now.

"This is Six! Put your people down in the shade and outa sight for awhile, over."

"Interrogative, Six: Is this pause permanent?"

"That's a negative! I'll let you know when we're moving again."

They couldn't stay — this wasn't the last objective of the day — it wasn't over yet. The bennies were melting away in the heat — the sweet, sweet bennies. Bravo hadn't humped enough today to satisfy somebody.

How does a person tell someone over and over that the word has been changed, the word has been changed? "What do you mean we ain't staying here — what are you passing that bum word for?"

"You heard it — they changed the word again."

"Well, just how fucking far we gotta hump today, anyway?"

"I don't know, but you better get some shade now while you got the chance."

Two minutes later the words most hated by the grunts were passed around the hill: "Saddle up, we're moving out. Pass it on."

So the grunts moved on but this time they were without the thing that was essential to sustain a tolerance of the Nam — they didn't know where they were going anymore.

"Hey, how come we couldn't stay on that hill back there, how come we gotta leave?"

"I don't know. I guess the dart didn't land on that hill, that's why."

"What dart?"

"Them fucking heavies back in their air-conditioned bunkers at Quang Tri just sit there drinking beer and throwing darts at the map. That's how they decide where we're going, Studly."

"Oh, yeah? My old man would never believe this shit, never."

Sanity was becoming a thing of degrees. The bigness, the infinity of a wide-open landscape, the sense of utter freedom in moving in this space loosely bounded by blue-white sky and green-red earth was leaving. The farther the grunts humped the smaller it all became. The world was taking on the smallness, the heavy limitations of an asylum. Under the heat the mind started to wander easily, began bouncing freely between fantasy and reality.

If you lived in Arlington you'd be home by now. Nevah hoppen, GI. Here's the church and here's the steeple open the doors and here's the gooks. Spare the rod and spoil the child. Spoil the rod and spare the child. Spoil the spare and rod the child. Step right'up and win a nice tall glass of cold . . . If you saw a waiter in half you'll find old menus, broken china, tips, pencil stubs . . . .

"Christ — talk about busting heavies . . . ."

Amelia Earhart lives. Pigs can fly too and through rain with goggles on. Body count wart count who gives a flying fuck count. We must recognize that the grotesque is commonplace and the commonplace grotesque . . . .

"This is Six! I'm hearing too much talking and noise back there — get them quiet and keep them spread out, over."

"Why the fuck don't he tell me something important? Something like, tonight half the stars in the sky will be hung upside-down? Something important for a change. Spread it out — I'll spread it the fuck out, all the way back to the goddam World."

Whatever you do don't be a wallflower at an orgy. In sickness and in health til death do us a job with liberty and defecation for all. Yippy skippy fuck. No wonder then that in a recent poll only fifteen percent of American Indians sampled wanted the U.S. to get out of Vietnam while over eighty percent wanted it to get out of America. Oh, the world's too wonderful for anybody in it to be this tired, this pissed off. What's it like to be drunk for ten years, Swifty? Jesus take my hand and lead me through. Jesus, let go of my hand you slimey puke. Winter uniforms will be worn as of Wednesday at 0600. All personnel are advised to be prepared for the change . . . .

It just went on and on with no regard for logic, with the sun getting low. "Six, this is One. Be informed we gotta heat casualty up here, a real one, over."

"What do you mean heat casualty? Who says he's a heat casualty? You gotta doc up there? Get the guy's temperature."

"We got it. It's one-oh-four plus and he's unconscious and hot and dry, over."

"Well, leave a couple troops back to cool him off and go on ahead, we ain't got much time left, you know."

"Roger that, Six, but the doc says he's in pretty bad shape. I'm right here with him and he's gonna need some help."

"Well goddammit to hell! Okay, bring him back here and all of your people. It's getting kind of dark anyway, but we ain't calling in no medevac bird to tell the little guys and the world where we are, you got it?"

They were stopping for the night, actually ending the endless. Grateful wasn't the word for the general reaction. Captain Sam was alone with his reaction.

"Goddam heat casualties — they just think they're tired. I don't know where they find these non-hacking bastards they're sending over here lately. They don't learn discipline no more — can't push themselves a little. Then when they get zapped their damn old ladies want to know how I got them killed. That's right, they think I'm the one gets their kids killed!"

First Platoon came back from their point position with the heat casualty and Sam pointed out in the dusk where he wanted the defensive perimeter set for the night. A dozen yards away from Sam, the new Lieutenant Andrews lay back on muscles that had never been so sore, staring at a deep, dark sky. He was thinking how a few weeks before at this time of night he was sitting in a club in the rear, soaking up a cold beer. Back then he would sometimes hear the drone overhead of the old converted Air Force DC-3s — "Puff the Magic Dragon" — and the muffled staccato of their guns answering the call of a unit in trouble somewhere. He would join the handful who ambled out to watch it. "Anybody want to watch them get some?" They would sit on top of a bunker or climb one of the sentry towers around the perimeter and watch and listen through eyes and ears fuzzy with beer.

The scene, though witnessed dozens of times, was never less than incongruous — with a cold beer in hand, transistor radio on a sandbag whispering the latest Stateside tunes, they watched a battle at midnight less than two miles away, watched the area framed by red tracers where men worked and died to the accompaniment of sounds which at that very moment were provoking bodies to the boogaloo back in Frisco and Denver, Philly and Dallas. Andrews had seen the same bizarre quality of this war only once again since leaving the rear — when he joined the Company at Cua Viet. Two miles offshore a cruiser and two destroyers boomed their ordnance into the DMZ while fifty feet in front of him young Americans swam and got drunk in the sun. But there was none of that whacky incongruity left now. It was all hard, steel gray reality. And there was no beer to fuzz over the sensation of it.

Back in the rear, before being sent out to the field, the young troops just in from the States are full of questions about what it's really like out in the bush. "How bad's the humping and the heat?" Now, few questions and no naivete remained. Until this day they had seen adversity and suffering at a safe insulated distance — through the television tube. Now it was all very close, very much in focus. There would be no drinking fountain down the hall, no cool shower followed by liberty call, no warm girl after the ordeal. The many days of longing to return to the World with its empty, acquisitive lifestyle — empty but safe — began. Mercifully, no enemy came out of the night.

3

May Day

Up from a drugging called sleep. The parade resumed before there was any sun to burn off the dew on the elephant grass; fog held the draws and valleys. The day was May first; the Russians were putting on a parade, too. They would show the world their latest tanks and missiles. All Bravo Company would show would be a lot of guts and a lot of heat casualties. At least it was still cool. Forty-five minutes later dawn came across the lush and placid hills and valleys. For a few minutes it was easy to forget that so brutal and unbeautiful a process as war was being played on this same stage.

The grunts pushed on. They rounded corners in the terrain and vegetation, grunted up rises and hills, stumbled, fell and rolled down rises and hills, tearing trousers, slashing arms and legs. They stumbled into occasional clearings after hacking and swearing at the stubborn growth, but still it was there. That sun rode the sky as if it had always been there, on top of everything, as if it had never been night; it resented anyone daring to move when it ruled above.

The grunts were no longer in a geographical place named Vietnam. They were in a box full of adversity and suffering, all the things one could think of to complete the old phrase, "anything but that." But this box had no limits — they would walk but they would never reach the other side, the end. Now, in their exhaustion, the grunts were little men — tiny pieces of life plodding numbly through something that was anti-life, bouncing off each other, too tired to bitch and curse each other anymore, wanting to live a little longer, long enough to reach the other side of the suffering-box they were trapped in. The grunts were no longer young bodies carrying young attitudes. They were now the young newly made old; bodies carrying their own corpses of youth. Each had his very own corpse to carry and his very own Dachau or Buchenwald to endure under his jouncing, clanging, oven of a helmet-hell. There was no alternative to living it through, no alternative to pushing one's body, mind and the nostalgic mix of sunny yesterdays and plans made for bright tomorrows back in the World through this limitless hell, no alternative to watching and feeling this battering and erosion, this early aging.

Because of the previous day, the one hundred forty-seven bodies now carried too little salt, too little water, and too many torn muscles. And they didn't even have an idea where this day's objective was. The day before they had been told which of the hills they faced would be the last until the following day. They had been deceived then, with the word being changed twice, but at least for much of the day there had been something to look at and think, that's it, that there's the one. But not this day.

"Hey, Tripper, is that our hill?"

"I don't know, George."

"Which one is it? How the fuck far we going today, anyway?"

"I told you, I don't know. I don't even think nobody — not even Sam — knows. Just keep following that dude in front of you there. We'll make it."

"How in the fuck can nobody know. I mean somebody's gotta know, don't they? I mean there's gotta be at least one dude somewhere that knows, don't there?"

"I don't know, George. I don't know."

A new level of pain would be reached and explored this day. At first only a few noticed it but by noon something physical was felt by all. After several hours in the rising morning heat, the hands and feet were no longer sweating. Some would of course last longer than others, but the thing was becoming undeniable: dehydration was setting into these one hundred forty-seven young bodies. The sweat still came out on the forehead, to run down and sting the eyes, but in a few more hours, thighs, chests, and backs would be drained, wrung dry, and more of the priceless water from near-empty canteens would be needed to keep the body temperatures of the flushed and unconscious below the level of death. The heat casualties started falling much earlier, fantasy wedged into minds much earlier.

I wonder if the gooks we're chasing get combat pay like us or maybe the birds get it . . . Whom the gods would destroy they first make Marines . . . You don't want to shoot me gook cuz if you kill me I'll be pissed off and so will Mom and Dad and all the guys I should be getting drunk with today instead of humping after your ass, gook . . . Oh, we bomb the grass good we sure do . . . Me a deputy of death — ha! I like flowers in the spring and passionate broads in the dunes . . . .

"This is Six! I can see some of your people and they're all bunched up — now keep them the hell spread out, dammit."

Spread it out, spread it out — that's all he can say anymore. Smitty, spread it out . . . I know I'll impersonate an angel then the Captain can't find my ass to chew next time he gets bored . . . Hey, anybody know the death rate from breast cancer among beagles and bald eagles? . . . What size bras do beagles wear? . . . All the bombs and bullets destroying all the bamboo villages and bamboo people . . . They ought to take all the cash they spend on bombs and subsidize poets and painters . . . There'd be no such thing anymore as a poet being a pauper — never — and it'd be a better project than burning up babies . . . And peace under me peaceful over me peaceful before me peaceful after me peaceful . . . .

"This is Six, we'll be coming up on this objective here pretty soon.

Have your people follow second platoon on up and take from four to eight on the perimeter, over."

Now there could be the chance for some shade, something resembling a reward for enduring those last thirty hours. It took an hour for Bravo to get situated on the new hill. The main body was settled in less than fifteen minutes but for almost another hour small groups straggled in, carrying and dragging those claimed by the heat. The first priority on this hill was the clearing of a landing zone. A chopper would then be called in to take out the worst of the heat casualties and the man with the badly sprained ankle. Sam couldn't be slowed down anymore, which meant this hill was not a real objective. Bravo would have to move again in a short while. The questions multiplied; they came to sound more like the pleadings of the condemned.

"How long we gonna stay here?"

"Can we put up shade hooches?"

"How much farther we gotta go today?"

"We gotta get some water pretty soon, Sarge — my squad's down to less than half a canteen a man and them two new guys ain't got any left."

After a rest of thirty minutes, first, second, and weapons platoons went on ahead with Sam to the next hill. Battalion was getting itchy — their sacred time schedule was not being met as the pogues in the air-conditioned bunkers had planned, so Sam would have to take a chance and split his Company. After clearing the LZ and sending the "non-hackers" out on the bird, third platoon would saddle up and rejoin the Company.

When the chopper touched down it discharged the last person in the whole division the grunts expected to see — the battalion Chaplain. Only a very few were glad to see him. Chaplains are considered by most marines to be largely useless appendages on the corpus militaris. They're always acting a little too friendly to be for real, and when the bullets start flying what good is some guy babbling about the *Twenty-Third Psalm*? This day, however, the grunts would change their minds about chaplains, for not only had this one bothered to leave his air-conditioned chapel to come out and try to cheer them up a little, but this member of the general's "God Squad" was actually going to hump with them, share the merciless heat with them.

56

This second hump of the day proved short, only about 1100 meters, but it cost the grunts dearly in terms of water, endurance and morale. Third platoon, with the Chaplain, started out at 1:30, which meant this move would take them right into the hottest part of a hot day. The major part of the distance was covered in less than an hour; it was downhill and the trail had already been cut by Sam and the others. Only two stops had to be made.

Earlier in the morning those who were better disciplined and still clear thinking realized the Company would need a new source of strength, a new source of water. Most of the grunts were down to less than one canteen, and that would not last until the next morning. Finally, American ingenuity had bored through the predicament: why not drink one's sweat instead of wasting it on a bush towel or a sleeve? To those in a "normal" environment, the idea sounds absurd, pathetic, revolting. But to the grunts of Bravo, having their brains baked through on this May Day, the idea of drinking their own bodily secretions was greeted with enthusiasm in most, exhilaration in some. Another trick had been discovered to help them endure the agony of the sun, the agony of a craving which all but a very few Americans need never concern themselves within seven decades of life.

So they wiped their foreheads and licked their fingers. They raised a hand and ran the other up the hairless inside of the forearm, then drank the trickle of sweat that coursed down over the webbing of skin connecting thumb and forefinger. But now, two and three hours after, it didn't seem like such a good idea. The urea, dirty salt and carbon dioxide they took in produced dizziness and nausea in empty stomachs. They had to stop now to vomit, to throw up what could have been eliminated in a more logical manner hours ago. But there was damn little logic left in Bravo Company this afternoon. They kept drinking their sweat, some hoping they could get sick enough to get a medevac bird back to an air-conditioned hospital ward for a couple of days of rest.

After an hour on the move the grunts were at the bottom of the objective hill. They could see the rest of the Company sitting around on top of it. They could also see that it was going to be a bastard to get up — it was steep, at least forty-five degrees, and it was bare of any growth. When those who vomited regained a sense of balance, they stepped out of the shade and started up. A bare dirt path with no jungle to cut through was usually regarded as a benny by the grunts. But on this day the bare hill-side acted as a mirror for a garish sun. The earth came to look like a desert, the brightness erasing the reassuring horizon line; thirst and head-aches worsened. The grunts leaned into the hill for a step, two, three — and slid back down in the bomb-loosened soil. They tried again and again, clawing, cursing, pleading. If there is a hell, this is what it must be like — scratching up an endless hill bare of life, falling back, scratching and crawling back up a few feet, falling back again. A perpetual exertion with no perception of progress.

> *... Sing, vulture, sing your sweet song of death, of relief from all the bullshit of human existence, of muddling on, passing our failure on to each new generation ... on page four, delete para fifty-six and insert the following in lieu thereof: Fifty units of blood consisting of the following groups and types for the West Pac program ... PRO-GRAM! ... Who the fuck's in charge of the West Pac PROGRAM?? ... What crooked path of reasoning was followed by what breed of yawning fools to declare an operation to this useless goddam country justifiably necessary ... I hear the blare of barbaric trumpets, I see bronze rivers lapping marble shores ... barbaric blaring bronze marbles ... marble whores on marble shores*

But they made it up the glaring and endless hill, and then they huddled together in clusters of three and four, all trying to crawl under one green bush towel to get out of that sun for a few minutes, seconds. Hands cupped over eyes and ears in disbelief that they were really going through this.

Something about war was becoming very clear now. It was not the drama of one side named Us against the other side, called The Enemy. There was more to it than that. War in the middle of the twentieth century in Vietnam was a constant fight to survive against heat, thirst, poison-ous centipedes, endless humps, spreading jungle rot, sunburn, chapped and cracked lips and noses, twisted ankles, dehydration, intricate and constant patterns of pain from joints and muscles, unimagined extremes of bore-dom and exhaustion, stupid rumors about mad tigers that pounce on inattentive Americans at night, too few letters, too little food and booze and women, too much diarrhea, and too much despair that all this shit would never end, that home would never be seen again. The timeless and varied horrors of war were being freshened up and passed on to the newer, greener generation. "Come on, kid, you can make it."

Even the quiet and strong felt that something should be said and done about these maddening moves that began before there was any light on the day and went on and on with no reward; this humping for what seemed like nothing but the sake of humping. "Sir, I'm not in the habit of bitching or anything, but this crap is kicking my ass."

All but one of the not-so-strong stared blankly at the twitching calf muscles, at the blank, nerveless masks on other faces, at the great green oven that confined them. The one pulled his green undershirt up over his head and babbled to no one and everyone, "I can't go anymore, I can't, I can't — leave me here, go on, go on . . . ."

And now, piling on top of all that, exacerbating all this adversity, came the snap and whine of rifle fire racing through the valleys, across ridgelines and into burning ears. It had a muffled, down-below sound to it. Somebody had caught somebody in a low spot between two hills.

All the platoon commanders rushed up to Captain Sam to see what this latest piece of action was, the one their platoons were now least prepared for. "All right now, loyal lieutenants and staff NCOs, I'm gonna pass these binos around and you look down there to your left front, three fingers to the right of that there light green patch. You'll see dear old dying Delta getting their ass kicked but good!"

The only other rifle fire heard on this new op had been when Americans and ARVN had trapped some NVA between a pair of hills on the first day. Now it was the other way around. One of Sam's sister companies, Delta, had stumbled into an NVA bunker complex on the ridgeline parallel to Bravo's. The heat had rendered both companies equally unprepared to face enemy fire; something or somebody just decided that on this day it was Delta's turn. Sam provided a tragic running commentary.

"There's three more just went down — three marines that is. Shit, there's whole squads just running around like chickens with their heads cut off . . . don't know where they're going, nobody leading, don't know where the gooks is at. I can't get their captain on the hook . . . must have got him and his radioman both. There's supposed to be fixed wing and artillery on the way but they need something down there to hold them off until it gets here. Nobody's organizing nothin' down there . . . nothing."

Sam took advantage of the scene to make an example: "Take a good look at that crap down there and let it be a lesson to you — That's what happens when a unit loses its head. Look at them taking all them casualties for no damn reason, and only a few on our side shooting back. Can't even hear a friendly machine gun firing at them bunkers, can you?"

"We going down there, Captain?"
"Shit, you know we'll be going down. We're the closest friendly unit."

Sam kept watching the action he longed to join. He studied the terrain between himself and the firefight, turning over in his warrior's mind alternate approaches to the scene and various tactics to use once he got there. But the radio kept its silence through the long minutes. When a call finally came, it proved the greatest possible morale-raiser to the other one hundred forty-six. It was battalion reporting that a re-supply chopper was finally on the way out. While the grunts had waited and huddled under the green bush towels and poncho liners and while they listened to one of their sister companies get shot up, one of the world's few humanitarians in the rear got off his fat ass and loaded up a chopper with not only water but — it shouldn't have been true — mail! There would be relief at last from the sun, and there would be those perfumed pieces of paper called letters — reminders, confirmation that humping and sweating and losing hope were not the only things being done at this time on this planet.

While Sam watched the shooting and the dying, the grunts bent all their attention to their mail. They tore it open and studied over and over the words written by feminine, parental, brotherly, sisterly, or wifely hands. The packages full of Hershey bars and canned hot dogs and peaches and apples and peanuts and homemade cookies and cakes were passed around the hill. The few in each platoon without letters or packages collected and filled all the canteens, first dividing the number of canteens into the number of gallons and quarts in the steel cans, then measuring and pouring the precious liquid as carefully as if it were liquid gold, or radioactive. It came out to one-half canteen per man.

Sam got the call to move about twenty minutes after the water and mail came in, after eight more heat casualties were sent out. The bennies were always temporary. The platoon commanders went up on top for one last look through the binos and to hear the Captain's plan. First platoon would move out first, to act as a reconnaissance element for the rest of the company and to cut a trail. The surprise was not that they were moving but that they were not being sent to link up with and assist Delta Company. Stay on the adjacent ridge, and maintain observation of Delta was the way battalion had put the message.

Lieutenant George Sorenson and his first platoon moved out at ten minutes after three in the afternoon. A meteorologist could prove with his records of hourly and daily temperatures that the sun had now moved west far enough so that the temperature was starting the daily decline that would continue until about three or four the next morning. But exhausted and partially dehydrated grunts could hardly be expected to perceive such changes. To them it was still just plain "hotter than fuck and rising."

Sorenson's people went out "light," which meant they were leaving their new water behind for a couple of hours. The other platoons, never too thrilled about doing the work of others, would bring the five-gallon plastic water bottles onto the new objective later. To psych his men up for this next move, Sorenson told his squad leaders they were being cut a hus by the Captain by being selected to move out first. But as it would turn out, everyone would be equally tired that night, first platoon from hacking a new trail and the others from humping the extra weight of the water bottles. Not only were the bennies always temporary but they were usually exaggerated as well.

Even as first platoon was heading out, few grunts knew there would definitely be another move today. As they read the letters and drank the new water they hoped and begged within their own minds harder than they had ever hoped and begged before that "Yes, we're staying here tonight. He's looking out for us, he'll take care of us. We're staying!" But in no one's mind was there enough hope to crowd out the fear that squad leaders would come around again with the hated "Saddle up!" The uncertainty, the word changes were getting as bad as the thirst.

When it was passed around, the saddle up provoked groans and bitches loud enough to be heard in the next province, and it gave Lance Corporal Bill Finney his first chance to show some initiative; to be heard. Two months before, on his third day in the Company, Finney had written on his helmet something that he hoped would tell the world just who William T. Finney really was; just how gung-ho he was: "Yea, though I walk through the Valley of the Shadow of Death I will fear no evil, cuz I'm the meanest motherfucker in the Valley!"

During the previous two days Finney had wondered about the constant humping and about the incomprehensible mechanism back in the rear that kept producing that one solution to the problem of the war: "Tell Bravo Company to move again." This low-ranking warm body in the hierarchy of the military and of life had reached some conclusions in his thinking and now he wanted to share them with everybody of every nationality within range of his voice.

"Why the fuck we gotta move again? Why the fuck don't we just sit down and let the gooks come to us? You know what them gooks are doing now? Right this fucking minute, Man? Half of them are sitting on a hill watching us and laughing, and the rest of them are blowing fucking Zs in a fucking hammock is what they're doing. That's right. While we bust our ass humping these fucking hills. But that's all right 'cuz we're big tough marines — we can hump all day and fight all night. Then at night when we're tired and blowing Zs they come out and overrun our ass. That's when we find the little bastards — at night — when we ain't ready for them. Not now in the daytime. Real fucking smart. Real unfucking believably smart!"

Oh, how the grunts could swear! The four-letter words came out of the young faces as smoothly as they flowed from a forty-year-old whore's mouth in a Singapore alley. It lost its profanity, even started to sound a little beautiful against the absurdities of the day.

Lance Corporal Finney's brand of analysis was now the norm in the Company. Among the few still capable of building their complaint around logic was the head corpsman of the Company. Doc Sellers intercepted Lieutenant Andrews and issued a reasoned appeal. "Lieutenant, you gotta talk to Six now. These guys can't take this much moving in the heat. Talk to him, will you?"

The Doc could not yet accept the fact that there was no real alternative to the madness of the day, that while there were valid, medically sound

62

reasons to say no to the latest order, the move had to be made. "Well that's it — I'm gonna just tell Six we ain't going anywhere for a couple days. Battalion can go fuck themselves — court-martial me. I give a shit now." Sellers walked up to the top of the hill, stood next to Sam and looked down in the direction of the firefight, the dying, for several long seconds. Without saying a word, he turned and walked back down the hill.

Now it was back to the bush, back to licking sweat off arms, sucking buttons, back to trying to hold onto consciousness.

. . . There's a left-handed banana tree over there Gunny. The Defense Department says thirty-one percent of all military personnel wear glasses, and everybody else would rather wear bell-bottoms and Afros. How's the West Pac program now? Tell Ma I'm coming home and Judy Jingleboobs . . . .

Now the grunts were just leaning forward, trying to get a leg and foot out in front before they fell. There was no sense in thinking about how one got into this activity and how and when one would get out of it. Time no longer figured in the equation of it all. Every grunt, every man everywhere, was born into this mindless trudging in the heat, and every man everywhere would die still involved in it. Dreams were illusions, one's last day in Vietnam was an illusion, ambitions and plans to pursue back in the World were illusions, so why make up any more? All the grunts really had out here in the hot green maze was a sense of mutual dependence, of belonging to the next few minutes of each other's lives.

The television generation was getting its view of the world smashed today. From the boob tube they had learned that for every problem there is a simple, instant solution. With the right pill you can banish acid indigestion or the aches and pains of fatigue. With the right deodorant, one need never fear social ostracism or unpopularity. And if you're pressed for time, throw in a TV dinner. Here the grunts were, though, faced with a new one that wouldn't go away. They had been gulping water and Kool-Aid and salt tablets, frantic to relieve an agony that defied relief. Slowly the hard reality came through: there was no alternative, no time-out, no falling out from this "field problem." All this would have to be endured — second by second, minute by superheated minute, with no excuses from mother good enough to get one out of it. The grunts were being beaten to a psychological pulp. The dream of returning to the great dreamland America was looking more hopeless every minute.

... Please excuse Johnny from dressing for gym today. He has a sore ear and the doctor said ... Oh Christ, what if the gooks hit us now? Goddam don't let them hit us now! Too quiet here, too quiet, no cheers. The broads in short skirts that ride up their thighs when they jump around are supposed to be cheering us out here. We're about to score — only a little farther. Nobody to cheer for us out here — nobody to call a foul on the Nam for fouling us like this. The Nam is the biggest goddam foul that ever was. No such place as the World — all a big joke — never going back, it all blew up ... Think of hearses and milk ... whores and mist ... pissed, I'm pissed ... let us go, Lord, back to driving around to the hamburger joints ... the Frenchies knew how to fight a war; sent over gallons of wine, clean whores and doctors for them ... that's the way to do it, but not for us — we're civilized ....

The grunts couldn't believe it but two of the five-gallon water bottles second and third platoons were carrying for first sprang leaks during the move. Five gallons of water are heavy, whether one is rested and healthy or exhausted and dehydrated, and so some of the troops had probably helped a sharp branch puncture the plastic bottles. Maybe so, maybe not; anyway the bottles were getting lighter with each step.

... Green, green, everywhere green ... the green of the Nam wears off on humping through the green shit ... when the green grunts fall down they drop their ketchup bottles and say ouch and get ketchup all over themselves ... all over the ground and the kitchen floor and the green Nam ... the redder they get, the redder the ketchup flows and then they don't say ouch any more ... red on green ... mothers cry ... mothers cry ... fathers ask why ... fathers ask why ....

Bravo came up on the last hill of the day in the final fifteen minutes of daylight. The last two platoons in the column were still moving as dusk turned into darkness and, predictably, contact with them was lost twice. And just as predictably, something else intolerable happened — an accidental discharge. In his exhaustion somebody forgot to put his grenade launcher on "safe." Somebody's finger slipped from trigger guard to trigger, and no pair of ears could miss the deep "thunk" as the grenade left its tube and bored into the dirt an inch away from somebody else's heel. It had not traveled far enough to arm itself so the grenade didn't blow, and the heavies didn't have to try and explain to two more pairs of parents how it was their own sons' stupidity and not a human wave attack by the fanatical NVA that cost them their legs and eyes and sanity. But Sam couldn't be bothered by such elementary screw-ups now. He had to have a meeting before they were too far into the night, before the fog came in to carry their voices farther than they already carried, to plan for tomorrow, for the contact with the enemy his Company would surely face, the combat he longed for, thrived on. The grunts were left to dig in wherever squad leaders thought best.

"I understand the water bottles broke on the way over here. That wasn't too bright, letting them get broke like that. That shit don't go in this Company. First platoon needs their water same as everybody else. They didn't get none from that last bird this afternoon. So, second and third platoons, before you hit the rack tonight you go around to your people and collect some from everybody to give to first. I want that expedited with no noise, and before it gets too dark. And don't let something like this happen again. That should be all I ever have to say on that situation.

"I got a message here for you, second platoon, just come over the battalion net. Some hospital in Mitchell, South Dakota, reports Mrs. Joe Belknap gave birth to a baby boy two days ago. Six pounds, eight ounces, both doing fine. Make sure you tell Belknap tonight right after you go back from here.

"Okay, now I want you to listen to the rest of this good now. I know the troops are tired after these last two days but it might even be worse than that tomorrow. You probably guessed we're going down to where Delta got their ass kicked. I got a call from battalion here a while back telling what their casualties were. They had nine killed down there and eighteen wounded. One of the KIAs was the Company radioman and one of the WIAs was the Company commander. You saw what a cluster-screw that outfit was. It only took ten gooks to fuck that Company up that bad — that's all battalion says there was — ten gooks. That ain't gonna happen to this Company. Tomorrow morning we're gonna sweep that hill and clean out that squad of gooks. Battalion's giving us all day, there won't be anymore of that rush-rush shit for awhile. We're gonna take our time and do it right. This thing's gotta be expedited right so we don't lose nobody for no unnecessary dumbass reason, like Delta did. Now tomorrow morning about seven we'll lead outa here with first platoon, weapons, second and third, down that same finger we just came up. About halfway down . . . ."

So while Captain Sam ended his day by reporting the beginning of life in one country far away and planning the end of life in this one, the platoon sergeants and squad leaders of Bravo ended theirs by crawling around in the night, collecting capfuls of water from everyone to make up for what had been lost on the afternoon hump. First platoon was down to one half canteen for every two men. They would need more than that to be ready for the next day, to do what had to be done, but neither they nor anyone else would get it.

The rest of the grunts ended their day by "lightening" their packs. It was an exercise that had more to do with mental health than weight. They laid out in the darkness everything they carried and picked out what could be left behind. Certain essentials, of course, could not be thrown away — water, food, ammunition. There was something illogical but necessary in all this, for what could be taken out and thrown away weighed only a few ounces while what could not be discarded totaled anywhere between thirty and seventy pounds. Old letters, extra books of matches, odd lengths of rope, pretty stones from the dry streambeds were the things taken out and not re-packed.

Just the act of picking up something and saying to oneself, "I'll never have to carry this again," was a source of considerable relief, something close to exhilaration. It was confirmation that one still retained some say about his future. Sam and the Colonel didn't own every minute of these one hundred twenty-eight lives, not every single last minute. "Do I want to carry these extra bootlaces anymore? Fuck no!" A few grunts held a more liberal interpretation of expendable. Here and there in the darkness a trooper slipped a grenade or a couple of trip flares under a bush or a pile of damp leaves and dirt. His load for tomorrow was now 1.1 pounds lighter. And PFC Behl even got rid of the smelly, shriveled ear of his first victim.

After Sam's meeting, after the water for first platoon had been collected and awarded, one hundred twenty-eight bodies, pushed beyond exhaustion and moved by little more than the inertia of a stubborn pride, lay back on poncho liners on a damp hill. The grunts now had the feeling something had been taken out of them that could not be replaced. Eyes played over the stars and picked out familiar formations, the ones learned in grade school. It was the first time those forms had really been looked at since grade school. There was beauty up there, out there dozens and hundreds of light years away. It was all so clear, so clean — white dots on a blue-black infinity — cleaner than a desert. The mind cleared in the cool night, then embraced peace as fog walked into the draws and valleys, giving the hills ghostly halos.

... Before me peace ... under me peace ... over me peace ... after me, there must be peace ... do we belong here? ... we're in harmony with nothing ... we scar and crater the earth here ... we enhance nothing ... in harmony with nothing ... nothing ... nothing ....

4

The Best Years of His Life

The first thing the grunts noticed about May second was that the sun came up again. To truck driver and scientist alike, "normal" people back in a "normal" world, that development was less than elementary. To brains and perceptual organs that had been folded, spindled, mutilated, and baked for two days it was something to note — this day could easily turn out to be another day of seeing dreams die in the heat waves, of craving what couldn't be had, of putting one foot in front of the other and feeling the squinching shock of tibias crashing against femurs. And added to all of that shit, there would probably be the enemy today. It had all the earmarks of one of those days when the closest thing to local amusement would be watching the attrition of youth.

By seven o'clock Sam had enough daylight to send out his point. The column snaked back down the trail it had cut the night before and made a turn to the right at about two hundred meters. Gradually downhill for three hundred more meters, up a sharp little rise and they were on it, the hill connected with the one where Delta Company had been chewed up the day before. The grunts had a perfect view of the NVA bunker complex, a cluster of a dozen little dirt mounds with eyes; mounds that would have so much to say about the tomorrows of one hundred twenty-eight lives. Sam would leave all his machine guns and mortars here with a reserve force of one platoon to act as a supporting base of fire. It was only nine o'clock in the morning but already the sun and the two previous days were cutting into the one hundred twenty-eight. Eight had to stop and get under some shade before they could go; six finally had to be dragged or carried in by buddies. Two others had slipped on leaves and brush still wet with fog, fallen back down the hill and ripped open arms and thighs on bamboo stalks. But Sam didn't want to hear about heat casualties, sprained ankles and cuts this morning. He sat behind a bush and studied the enemy bunkers through his binos.

"I don't see no movement down there but that don't mean they're not there still. Then again they might have left last night. I thought I heard some digging a couple times. Anyway, the machine guns will be set up right here where they can see all of them bunkers. We'll lead outa here with first and second platoons. Third'll be the reserve back here around the gun pits. First is gonna go down over that way and on around the back of the hill until they link up with that platoon of Delta's that's waiting there. They'll be the blocking force for second sweeping around the face of the hill and through the bunkers. We want to force them bastards down and out in that clear area right down there. Then the mortars and machine guns will work on them."

It went perfectly, better than an assault staged for the heavies back in the States. Forty minutes after Sam passed the word first platoon was around in position with the platoon from Delta, and second platoon was beginning their sweep. The machine guns rained through the bunker complex. Then the grunts walked through it, rifles on automatic. No enemy appeared. They had left the night before, carrying off their dead and

70

wounded through the draw between the two Marine companies, back to a haven in the north.

Disappointed and angry at the missed chance, Sam called battalion for new orders. Destroy the bunkers and call back when it's done was the new directive. And onto it was added something more obligatory than a direct order, something not to be repeated any more than was necessary. American military units take pride in the tradition that they never leave their own dead and wounded on the field of battle. Yesterday Delta had violated that tradition; six men could not be accounted for after the casualties had been counted and sent back to the rear. Sam and Bravo were told to find the six men, or bodies, before nightfall.

The platoons pulled back, shuffled positions and assignments and waited for Sam's next word. Second and third would blow the bunkers and look for the MIAs. On the fifteen minute move down from the mortar position to join Sam, the third platoon was suddenly hit very hard by the heat, now moving over ninety degrees. Of twenty-three who started out to join the second platoon, only fourteen completed the short move. Several were legitimate heat and exhaustion casualties, doubling over and vomiting salt tablets. But several just doubled over moaning "I can't go on no more, no more . . . ." Their bodies were close enough to dehydration to preclude tears.

Sam had his second and third platoons in position on the north slope of the hill by two in the afternoon. They moved out three minutes later. During an operation like this any one man could hold up the entire formation if he saw something that should be checked out in some detail. Things were bad enough with the heat and the brambly undergrowth, but the stopping, moving and stopping again only compounded the frustration. Each bunker was fired into, then torn apart by hand, then the next and the next.

"Hold it on the right. I said hold it the fuck up dammit, we gotta check one out up here."

"Get down, we're gonna blow it."

"No, don't frag it. You'll hit your own people."

"You gonna blow that thing up there or not?"

"Just kick in the top and sides."

"Well shit, do something dammit, let's get this fucking thing over with."

"Okay, move it out, go ahead. Go on."

Third platoon had fired on and torn up two bunkers and second, farther up the slope, had destroyed three when Carl Andrews stopped the formation. He had come to something at the bottom of the hill in the dry streambed that should be checked out. The glare of a mean sun off white rocks blurred the area until they were only a few feet from it. Scattered over the streambed and up the far slope were eight rifles, two pistols, two corpsmen medical kits, blood-soaked boots, bandages, trousers, shirts, flak jackets, dented and shot-through helmets, and piles of spent cartridge cases. Here was one of the places where the NVA had cleaned up the previous day; one of the places where the Delta grunts had run around like chickens with their heads cut off and paid for it.

Andrews, his radioman, and another grunt walked across the littered area and up another dry streambed. They found and followed a blood trail but it disappeared in the rocks and brush after a few meters. There were no bodies in the area, Vietnamese or American, no sign of any of the shallow graves the NVA dig to confuse the American body counters. Andrews called the information back to Sam and the sweep continued.

The sun slid past three-thirty, three-forty-five, four o'clock and the grunts pushed on. They stumbled and fell ahead through the most maddening mix of "wait-a-minute" vines and elephant grass to be found in all of Southeast Asia. All of it, the worst jungle growth in the Nam was right here on this north slope of this unnamed goddam hill. The whole adverse mass seemed to congeal and produce a swimming-through-water sensation. Another hour and still more heat and it turned the water to oil. Another hour and yet more heat, and the oil became grease — stroking through grease with only fog in view where a destination should have been.

The NVA were right, it was a good place for bunkers and an ambush. This was how Delta had found the enemy the day before. Too tired to lift legs anymore, they had leaned forward and fallen into the tangled vines, stood up and fallen ahead into them again until they were twenty — or maybe only ten feet — away from the barely-visible bunkers. Then the AK-47s came alive, on automatic. They had been close enough for the NVA to watch the young American faces register that ultimate oh-God-no-not-now-not-me surprise, fear, pain, and then the resignation in death. But all of that was yesterday. Today there was everything but the enemy.

Here and there a grunt would fall ahead into the brush and not get up.

He just lay there staring and panting into the green viney cage around his head. He would stay down until a buddy came back to lift his arm and remind him he only had 42 or 96 or 173 more days to go and then he would never have to go without a cold drink, never have to walk everywhere he wanted to go. Corporal Randolph J. McAdam, who still had the strength to pick up his buddies and hump on, glanced over at his platoon commander and gave Andrews the most pointed and poignant lesson on The Meaning of War the latter would probably ever get. "Ain't this a hell of a way for a young guy to spend the best years of his life, Lieutenant?"

This day's events now had the effect of confirming in most of the young bodies and minds present that the war was, in fact, a massive intrigue to kill youth, the conspiracy of Things Old and Disappointed to bludgeon the hope and optimism of Earth's newest generation. Corporal McAdam was more right than any statesman in the world today — this was a hell of a way for a guy to spend the best years of his life — a hell of a way. This was not war as it was supposed to be enacted in the twentieth century. These were not scientist-diplomats in white jackets seated in swivel chairs at long consoles of buttons — buttons flashing in different colors, blip-blipping, whining like in the James Bond movies. These were last year's football players, pool-playing dropouts from down the block, drag-racing steelworkers' sons who got their girls in trouble at the drive-in movie on warm summer nights, crew-cut ranchers' sons from Kansas. To stalk the fanatical sons of North Vietnamese rice farmers and brick-makers they had no ICBMs or nerve gas or hydrogen bombs or Distant Early Warning systems; they had a couple of gadgets from the Colt Arms Company of Hartford, Connecticut, and then they had nerve endings and muscles and a few doctrines and reactions learned in training. They had damn little more than George Washington's grunts had.

So now today, May second, nineteen sixty-nine, the Big Day had finally arrived. Not the day of Armageddon or the Final Judgement but the day young dreams born of young minds — dreams of I-want-to-be-a-cowboy, and success, and not-a-care-in-the-bowl-of-cherries-world — would die. Some monstrous hairy-knuckled hand wielding a knobby club rode down these hot midday rays and battered, bludgeoned into the dirt all the dreams, the ambitions the grunts formulated back at All-American High while they gathered in that high-arching pass and streaked into the end zone to bring the crowd to its feet, while they watched young developing female bodies bounce and sway down the halls, while they heard commencement speakers describe the unlimited opportunities they would face in the next half-dozen decades.

These young bodies were being brutally reminded that they were fallible, that they could be made anonymous once again and forever. From now on, cheers would not follow the sweat. Here it was — bam bam whack! Tough shit, kid. Now it looked like one's Freedom Bird would never come. The whole damn planet and all of life looked like a lie now, there would be no end to this shit. The Freedom Bird and the States were all myths. They would never come true. And the myths were the President's gifts to all good grunts in the world; for Christmas, for New Years, for birthdays, for all days. Thanks for signing up anyway, kid. We had no way of knowing it would be all this bad, but thanks anyway — we needed the warm body. Carry on . . . above and beyond the call . . . with complete disregard for his own personal safety . . . carry on, kid.

Then it was over — over for the day that is — and the grunts knew there were no enemy near this hill. "This is Six! Send all your people up on top here to get some shade for awhile, all but a fire team or so, then you and that fire team come back along that streambed once more, see if you can't find them bodies. They gotta be around here somewhere."

So Andrews checked it over again, through the bloody and littered area, up the new trails and dry streambeds, but again there were no bodies to be found. Tomorrow morning six telegrams would have to be sent back to the World telling Mr. and Mrs. Schwartz, Jones, O'Donnell, Camacho, Gianatti, and Smolinski, that their sons were officially listed as Missing In Action. Six months later more telegrams would be sent out, changing the original message to Missing In Action and Presumed Dead.

The grunts humped onto the hill they had just swept, fell into the small patches of shade under bushes and trees, and got drunk on the idea of resting, of cooling off. Pretty soon Sam called again but it was not the hated saddle up order. Delta Company had given him a couple of cans of water and he wanted to pass it out before they humped the 200 meters back to their hill for the night. As they stood in line waiting for their half canteen cup of hot water a chopper circled in and dropped just the benny everyone dreamed of, craved: an external net full of green five-gallon water cans. The hump back would be easier now.

74

Sam gave the grunts fifteen minutes to savor the rest and the water before issuing his last saddle up for the day. No one was too tired to give the usual response.

"What the fuck's that saddle up shit? I thought we was staying here tonight. Goddam, how fucking far we gotta hump today?"

"Ah, it ain't so far back to where the mortars is at, only about two, three hundred meters at the most."

"Yeah, but that's two, three hundred too far now."

Already shadows were filling up the valleys and draws. This last hump of the day went slow but no one fell out — there was a guaranteed long drink of clean water at the end of this one. Back on the hill, with Bravo Company together again, Sam called a last meeting before nightfall. If a civilian could have witnessed this conference, he would probably report that these half dozen men in green were either rehearsing the rites of some primitive religion or asking the clouds for rain. Three of the six had temperatures over 102° and all were bending forward every few seconds to counter the now constant dizziness. The Captain reported that battalion had called again. There would be no more of the mindless humping in the heat for awhile. Bravo would be staying on this hill, actually sitting on this hill for at least another day. When this directive had sunk into one hundred twenty-seven skeptical heads there was once again reason to smile, even reason to use a little energy to laugh again. "Did you hear that, Man? We're staying, fucking staying! That's right, we ain't gonna do a fucking thing for at least two days the Lieutenant said. Not a fucking thing!"

Sitting in foxholes that night watching the moon, watching shooting stars and sipping the new clean water, the Freedom Bird and the World didn't look like lies anymore, at least not like the big lies they seemed this afternoon. Each grunt promised himself he would live through whatever this hot, hilly, green, wet land held in the next hour, day, week and ride his Freedom Bird away, away from all this bullshit forever — and not in a body bag but sitting in that soft seat staring at stewardess-bodies.

It was good to wake up after the sun was up, for a change. Damn good. And it was good to stand up and look at the deep green hills and draws all around and know these hills and draws would not have to be humped over today. That is, one "knew" that beautiful fact while the dark possibility of another word change hung in the back of his mind. The obscene scream of "Saddle up!" could still shatter the morning tranquility. But as the sun moved toward the midday point it was accepted that May third really would be a full day of slack; beautiful, skating slack. Very few in the Company even felt like expending the energy of thought and muscle involved in writing letters; raising a full canteen of water to one's mouth was enough.

The real beauty of this formerly small and simple act of drinking water was that it could be done with the realization that one was not limited to a capful, and it would not have to be squirted back into the hot canteen. You could take a whole damn mouthful and then you could either swallow it all at once or you could play with it as long as you wanted. You actually had a choice for a change — gargle it, squirt it around inside your mouth, let each tooth and taste bud savor it. Hell, you could almost have a damn orgasm right there on a mouthful of plain old water! Damn good, for a change. And for another change, the American grunts in Vietnam had something in common with the rest of their generation back in the World, for as they slushed that new water over hot, dry, gums and teeth and tongues, an uncountable number of Americans were walking down a hall, pushing a button and putting their mouths over a clear arching stream of water so cold it stung teeth. Life in the bush made the drinking of water one of the greatest of earthly pleasures, almost on a plane with sex.

A re-supply chopper came out in the late morning and dropped five recovered heat casualties from the day before and fifty cases of C-rations. That broke down to four new meals per man. Now another of the great pleasures of life was available.

While shrunken stomachs began working on the new water and food, the grunts went to work shoring up their attitude against whatever new adversity the next three days held. They tore apart all the gear they had to carry and looked for things to throw away, ways to lighten tomorrow's load. And after they had thrown away all the extra bootlaces and empty cigarette packages and extra matches and the pretty souvenir rocks, most of the grunts took a razor blade to their flak jackets and cut out some of the fiberglass plates. Here again, like the night before last, it was the act of discarding part of what they had to carry that sustained and lifted their now-initiated and hardened spirits. No matter that the plates they were throwing away might save them from a stomach full of razor-sharp, red-hot shrapnel in the near future. Just getting rid of something — anything — made them feel better, made tomorrow look a little more tolerable. It was worth the loss in protection.

With the pack-lightening completed, with nothing but slack to contemplate for the whole day, it was inevitable that reflection on what had been survived in the past three days of their very young lives would come over some of the grunts. The brutal exertion of the humps stretching over the last seventy-two hours was over, the heat was over for awhile, and the unbelievable sixty-five heat casualties and twenty-three medevacs without the aid of one booby trap or one round of enemy fire were over. The most horrendous three days in the histories of most of these one hundred twenty-eight lives were over. Now it was somebody else's turn, somewhere else, some other day.

Grunts are and always have been necessarily preoccupied with the here and now of their particular adversities. Throughout military history, of course, ordeals were endured comparable to that just completed by Bravo One-Three. But the grunts of Bravo would never consider any previous ordeal as worse than their own. The worst hump ever was the one just completed, the one that had lasted over the last day in April and the first two days of May 1969. For the next four or five decades they would remind each other and tell wives, children, grandchildren, and anyone else who would listen about the time "back in '69 in the Nam, or maybe it was '68 . . ." when they thought the humping would never end, and maybe a couple of firefights would be added to liven up the tale, but "We made it. Them old-timers back there might have done some sweating but whatever they went through, it couldn't have been as bad as these last three days, no way, Man."

Yesterday was yesterday and today would have to be hoped for all over again. The potential for a second slack day was as feeble as a newborn infant. It would have to be carefully nurtured, kept alive: don't step too fast, don't breathe too hard. So now, on days like May fourth, the grunt felt a strong need to do something to preserve everything about life as he knew it, from values and assumptions of an everyday familiarity to the most basic fundamental: sanity itself.

A grunt in the field is one of the most superstitious varieties of human life. Before he was sent to Vietnam there was a touch of the rational in him, or at least the desire to be somewhat rational, but during his year on the other side of the world, that rationality was pushed aside by events in which there was little or no reason. Frequent disappointment and disillusion caused by faulty intelligence, continuous word changes, and the ubiquitous uncertainty and fear pushed the grunt to erect around himself elaborate defenses consisting of no more than hopes, fears, and ritual acts. This delicate barrier was then positioned against the audial perception of that worst imaginable development — a sergeant screaming "Saddle up!" Aided by little or no prior experience with inductive, deductive, or any other kind of reasoning, the grunts arrived at some weird conclusions.

"Just watch — I bet if I eat this can of peaches now we'll move before noon. That's the way it's been happening every time after a bitching hump ever since I been here — just watch."

"Don't walk up there past Six's area now — it's too early. You get up and walk around and old Captain America's gonna think you want to hump some more, and he'll find some hill for us to hump to. Just stay down here quiet, get some Zs while you can."

That neither the battalion commander nor operations officer — the real originators of every saddle up — would ever have the time or inclination to study individual troops for evidence of hopes that required destruction never entered thought patterns low in the world's hierarchy.

When the two hated words finally did come at eight-thirty in the morning the first reaction was not that of having a dread confirmed, but relief that no more time would have to be spent sweating the situation. Just get your shit wired together and hump on out. Carry on — 129 more days. Carry on — 128 more days.

It wouldn't be a real long hump, but it wouldn't be a real skate either — about six or seven clicks. Platoons and people trailed out into the heat and green, a long line of green domes over squinting eyes. Soon the heat began to sink in again.

"Hey, Red Mountain, which hill is it — where we going?"

"Fuck, I don't know — just keep it spread out there."

"Yeah, well at least ask the Lieutenant can we take a break up here and get in the shade some."

"You know fucking A well you can't ask the man no dumbass question like that — let's go, Man."

78

In only the first hundred meters of the new move their bodies were reminding the grunts they were not doing something new, they were only resuming the old idiocy.

All the old bullshit was coming back now — spread it out, how far we gotta go, keep them spread out there, Tripper says there's a heat casualty back there. No, forget it, he's okay. Goddam, listen to me — every step — thigh bone crashing onto ground, dumb ground, takes shock sends it up to knee which hollers I can't last forever you son of a bitch. You better stop and let me blow Zs you son of a . . . . Thigh bone pushes, slams up into diaphragm flattens against lungs and the air rushes back up out past voice box and a desperate sigh-grunt "huh-huh" counts the clicks, ticks off the operations. Those damn heavies ought to make a "huh-huh" grunt count just like they make a damn body count and they ought to give a medal for every couple hundred grunts. Then everybody'd have a chestful and be a hero, even old J.S. Wragman. We're gonna fix them fucking heavies. Parts of this bullshit did not previously appear in The New Yorker. *I think how much I hate it, in a disinterested sort of way, then I come to hate so much I can't distinguish my consciousness as a witness of superficial temporal hatred. I come to embody extreme hatred. I am a hateful perception of my hateful self. I don't direct hatred at the exhaustion, the heat, or the gook I stalk — I become hatred. Something that produces hate and requires it to exist. I ingest it and excrete it, I taste hate of the hills, and of my base animal existence. Even that I have to fight, for I will never again have the luxury of taking anything for granted, as they say on Thanksgiving Day, like the fat Americans do all their lives, all their dullish barren sentences on earth. Stupid man, he warred a millennium ago and he wars now . . . . How much more my toenails and eyelashes hate it. I don't produce motion toward the next hill, I produce hatred; blue, turgid, agitated, surly hatred. Hatred almost beyond the control of anything structured to preserve sanity in a goddam brain housing group government issue, one each. Of those who have much, much is expected. Who the hell said that? The tendons under kneecaps protest the premature aging I impose, the hump imposes. They scream payback's a medevac motherfucker! I promise, I swear, I will not put them through such again — but tomorrow. How do you apologize to your body? It was made to use and God strikes dead those who fail to realize the potential He gave each. Who the hell said that? There is no goddam God — I rule my destiny! Hey Lieutenant, talk to the Captain will you, talk to him will you . . . .*

Through perceptions of madness and weak protest came the unmistakable sound of metal on metal ringing through the hills and the heat waves. It was a measured bam and a pause of three or four seconds, bam and a pause again. And between each bam was that smooth, darkly beautiful swearing. About fifty-eight men behind the point, the newest sergeant in Bravo, Jerry Buskirk, was practicing his newly recognized leadership ability. It was as big a test as he would ever face — looking for new ways to make humans do what they don't want to do. The technique he had decided on to deal with Private First Class Prentice Lichko was to bang him on the helmet with a machete.

"You worthless shithead, get up there, move it out. You ain't gonna lose contact with that man in front of you again. You will make this hump. BAM! Nobody's coming back after your ass if you fall out again, and quit your goddam whimpering. Too damn many of you guys think if you sweat a little a Freedom Bird's gonna pop outa the sky just for you. BAM! Well, it ain't gonna happen I keep telling you. We're gonna get up this damn hill before it gets really hot so we can blow some Zs for awhile. Fuck yeah, you'll have water, and Cs too. BAM! Move it there, you're losing contact. I ain't gonna get my ass jumped again today. Gotta save some for the Man to chew on tomorrow—not anymore today. BAM!"

At fifteen minutes before noon the rumors started taking on some substance, and they started traveling up and down the column a little faster. "I think this is the one we're going to. I heard somebody say it up ahead. Yeah, this might be it." Final confirmation came soon after: "Pass it back, the Lieutenant says this is definitely the one, right up there, for sure."

Here was the hill — goddam, at last here was the hill. It was this slope, the one they were leaning into, sweating over, cussing, not that steep bastard over there everybody was afraid it was. Right here, Baby, we're home.

"This is Six! Put your people around this thing from four to eight and put a fire team on this here knob you'll see to the south when you get up here." Second platoon was in, first platoon, then weapons, two squads of the third and last platoon. The celebration began. "Hey, Chief, Six says we're getting birds in with mail, rats and water, Man, fucking water!"

Lance Corporal Dennis Moy was beyond joining this or any other celebration. A few minutes before, the endless walking and the heat had completed the erosion of his *esprit de corps*, his sense of discipline and survival, enough to make sitting down where he was and refusing to go any farther seem not an act of insubordination, but the natural thing to do. And so he sat and stared, stared miles into the deep tangled green surrounding him and the rest of Bravo. A few of those filing by noticed and tried to encourage him to make it.

"Come on, Moy, let me give you a hand."

"Hey this is the hill, Man, you can make it. You're here already."

"Want a drink, a smoke?"

The encouragement had the tone of first the routine, then the curious, finally a vague fear. "Hey, Moy, let's go, Man — you hear me dammit? Hey, look at him — something's wrong. Go on in and get Doc back down here."

Corporal Manuel Rodriguez decided to stay down the slope with Moy. Rodriguez was a genuine "short-timer," with only fourteen days remaining in the Nam. He sat down next to Moy and started talking. Rodriguez had a real feel for anyone not as short as he. It wasn't really sympathy and he wasn't the kind to hold his experience over a newby's head the way some did. He just felt like doing something to soften the harsh reality faced by those with six, eight, ten months more to do.

Moy gave no indication that he heard anyone talking. As Rodriguez put a hand on his shoulder, Moy's every muscle came alive in an animalistic, ejaculative way. He turned on the corporal with red, violent eyes, screaming a language unrecognizable. He grabbed his M-16, clicked off the safety, aimed it at Rodriguez and sprayed the hill and sky with a full magazine. Every one of the eighteen rounds missed Rodriguez; it was one of those freaks of life and war after which the witness who should have been victim accepts without question the frailty of human existence. Rodriguez grabbed and sat on Moy until the first help arrived from the new perimeter.

"It's Moy — he's nuts — tried to shoot Wetback. You two take him up to the big CP, we'll get his gear. It's gonna be all right now, Moy. Come on it's all right. Get him in the shade and don't let him near anybody's weapon!" The nineteen-year-old Chinese-American was led, carried, dragged up the remaining few yards to the crest, still screaming, and was put under a poncho liner. Half of his body at least was now out of the sun. Moy stopped screaming after a few minutes but babbled on quietly to himself for hours, staring at nothing and everything. "Must have been the heat got him. You know I bet if he'd known how close he was he wouldn't have done it, you know?"

Rodriguez carried Moy's rifle and empty canteens up the rest of the hill and then he too sat in the dirt and stared, and wondered at the great mystery of this green place that decided who would walk again in familiar places and who would be carried home.

"Did you hear that? He was yelling in Chinese and he never even been to China, but his old man and old lady was there back before the Reds took over."

Helicopters were called but all were too busy for a routine medevac and the situation was not considered serious enough to warrant again giving away the Company's position. So Dennis Moy babbled on through the day, never eating, rarely drinking. The staring, the gibbering at the insanity of this business would go on into the night, the next day, the next night. America, the great insulator of her children from adversity, had cheated another of what was needed to live out this day.

At first, others were assigned to watch Moy on a rotating duty basis, two hours at a time, but soon the bond of common experience and a shared fate worked in over one hundred minds, and the grunts closed round their newest casualty. The feeling of this-could-happen-to-me dominated as they did all they could to relieve Moy of his hell. They gave him their Kool-Aid, their Hershey bars from home, showed him magazines, pictures of girl friends and sisters, they held his hand, cooled his face with a wet handkerchief, loosened his bootlaces and changed his socks, told him how nice he would have it in the rear. "Don't eat too much of that ice cream, Man, have a beer for every one of us." Two days after he fired at Corporal Rodriguez and the hills, a chopper arrived and Lance Corporal Moy was taken from the war.

"Screaming in Chinese and he never even been there, you know? Lucky bastard — now he's skating for a big man's ass."

*   *   *   *

While Dennis Moy lost his tenuous grip on the reality of heat and an unpleasant mission, other Americans back in the World were dealing with other realities. In Coraele, Georgia, Ernie Reber reached behind the desk in his insurance agency and turned up the air conditioner another notch; Mrs. Melvin Hildebrand of Denton, Texas, tried to remember if she had taken her birth control pill this morning; and Columbus Bowers sat on a john in the Greyhound bus terminal in Grand Island, Nebraska. He took a pen out of his pocket, crossed out a "Who needs niggers" and a "Back to Africa you black bastards" and scrawled his own "All white beasts eat shit — black is beautiful."

And in Beanville, Vermont, Rhonda Schimmel opened the oven door for a peek at her rising bread. Rhonda's husband Frank sells and services snowmobiles and other sports equipment in the Beanville area and, "Frank likes some homemade things to munch on after a hard day in the shop and I like to have some goodies ready."

In between saying hello and goodbye to her husband and caring for Sherry, three, and Dee Anne, twenty months (number three's due soon), Rhonda Schimmel has become something of an expert on yeast breads. "I've been teaching the girls in the neighborhood to make yeast bread and rolls. We also make a lot of sweet baked goods." Fortunately, no one in the Schimmel household needs to think thin, and calories don't count.

Florida natives who met and became high school sweethearts in Lake Worth, the couple married a year after graduation. Rhonda Schimmel began studies in nursing school but took a leave of absence when she got her ring. "We want to have all our children when we're young, and then we can all grow up together," she says. Husband and wife are twenty-three.

Next time you want to fill your kitchen with the aroma of love, try Rhonda Schimmel's bread. "I guarantee this recipe every time," she says. "One package active dry yeast. Beat with a spoon. Knead the dough. Punch out air . . . ."

5

The Third Herd

Now began a long dry time, a time when heat and boredom would dominate the bright days. For more than two weeks there would be no blood. There wouldn't even be the sound of distant gunfire. The humping through the green and heat would continue but it wouldn't have the frantic urgency of before. It was as if the battalion were slowing down its pace of life a little in order to more completely recover from Delta Company's disaster. In such a time a perversity was born, something that could only have a human brain as its source — the desire that anything, even a firefight, would occur to dilute boredom's acid-like eating away of optimism and youth.

Two hours after Moy's outburst, battalion called and told Sam that Bravo would keep their position for the next few days. The word spread fast and brought undreamed of relief. There was once again room for joy in life. "Kind of pretty, this little hill, ain't it?"

The company gunny collected all the explosive compound, C-4, carried by Bravo, took a squad onto the northwest edge of the hill and spent the next two hours blowing a landing zone. When no trees or brush over three feet above ground remained standing, the re-supply chopper was called in. Blowing the LZ was a race against the late afternoon darkness, but it was won. Everything fell from the sky this time — orange juice, socks, new canteens, gallon cans of pickles, tins of foot powder, cigarettes, grape juice, bootlaces, Red Cross kits of stationery, candy bars, toothpaste and brushes, chewing gum, razor blades, and "Oh Christ, that pilot better not drop it," one hundred twenty gallons of clean water in twenty-four marine green cans. It was a beautiful shade of green today. A new life-style was now possible and orders reflected it.

"Have your people shaved by noon tomorrow and tell them to eat up all their Cs — we gotta pallet coming in the morning."

The sounds now coming from the hill were more those of kids at Christmas than of men in war, as the grunts joked and joshed each other through the afternoon. Their joy was unbounded as they gorged themselves on rediscovered luxuries: the sharp sensation of toothpaste being brushed around in dry mouths, the ecstasy of taking and savoring a mouthful — a full mouthful — of clean water. Hands and feet could sweat again.

"Hey, Man, would you like the honor of sitting next to me and watching me smoke this entire cigarette, would you, huh?"

"Right on, Brother, right on your dying ass — I'm gonna have the honor of watching your face tomorrow when the bird brings the word and you read that Jody's come and got your sweet woman, ha! Got her right there while you're over here chasing gooks, oooo-weee!"

Of the dozen ambushes run in the next two days, no more than three or four were strictly ready to react, according to doctrine. On the rest, the grunts simply walked out to the designated ambush site, hid under the grass or brush and wrote letters, slept, or just lay back on the ground with eyes closed to contemplate the beauty of holding a mouthful of water, working it around with the tongue for ten minutes, twenty. At the end of the second day the squads and platoons came back up the hill to find the first sergeant with two long-awaited morale-raisers, mail and pay.

"Just like I said, Man, a letter for PFC Edward Haskins. Let's see if Jody's been snooping around that stuff. Open it, Man. Well, what she say, Man?"

"You just go fuck yourself, Joe Moore. She says everything is fine and the baby's still coming in about two months, and we're still getting married when I get home, so you and Jody can go straight to hell, Joe Moore, straight to hell."

"Well now, ain't that nice — she just afraid to tell you this week but wait'll next week, Man. Jody be done come and gone by then, you just wait — ha!"

Part of being a grunt is knowing when to prepare oneself mentally for the worst imaginable reality. Right now, after three full days on what had become known as Bravo Hill, Change 37, the worst reality imaginable was not death, but a resumption of those endless humps in the heat, pursuing an enemy who would not allow himself to be found or even seen. The grunts began to sense it individually and were almost afraid to reveal the common realization.

"Hey, ah, you know how long we been here now? I mean it's kind of unbelievable, ain't it?"

"Yeah, and my hooch is just getting comfortable."

The call from battalion came at about eleven in the morning; the hated frenzy of preparation was taken up again. The Company was caught at a time more awkward than usual: there was too much water and too many C-rations to carry. But a heroic effort was made to consume it all.

"Here, Man, drink the rest of this juice."

"I just drank half a fucking can. I drink anymore and I'll get diarrhea in five minutes instead of two hours from now!"

Every canteen, every plastic water bottle was filled but still there was too much of the precious water. Who among these men-children thought they would ever see too much water? Living the agony of thirst and heat-stroke, then gorging themselves on a sudden flood of water in the space of three days produced a mind-bending bewilderment on this morning in May. All knew they were engaging in the grossest sacrilege.

"Look at this shit, throwing away water. If anybody pulled this three days ago we'd have shot his ass!"

Captain Sam called up his platoon commanders, pointed them in the right direction and formulated a plan as he spoke.

"We'll lead outa here with second platoon, then the CP, weapons, and third. First platoon, you stay back to send the water cans out on this bird we just called in, then take off on the same trail we use. We won't get no more than a click ahead, then we'll wait for your lead people to link up. We're going to that hill that's got them two big craters on it. I want to be walking outa here in ten minutes."

In the next ten minutes, Lance Corporal Craig Billings and Private First Class Booker Carver Lincoln added a new twist to the preparations they had gone through so many times before. One of these grunts had, in the last two days, bent his every thought to avoiding a repetition of those first three days in May. By themselves such thoughts were not now uncommon in the Company, but the distance between thought and act was still considerable in all but these two.

"Hey, Lincoln, come here, pal. Hey listen, ah, how about paying me back that hus I cut you on your R & R?"

"Yeah, I'll pay you back, soon as this op is over. I gotta go pack and be moving in a couple of minutes."

"I mean now, Lincoln, right fucking now."

"How in the fuck I gonna pay you back now, out here?"

"Listen, Man, you and me start grab-assing, see, then I act like I get pissed and start throwing hands. Then you grab your E-tool and hit me in the foot, right here real hard, see?"

"Oh, that's real sweet, Billings, real fucking sweet. You get outa the bush, back with the beer in the rear but I'm still humping my ass off. Fuck that shit, Man."

"Ten bucks, Brother Books . . . Twenty bucks, Books . . . Twenty-five . . . ."

The first corpsman to look at Billings' ankle knew what the deal had been. Not only the mastermind of the plan but Lincoln too got out of the next few humps. Both were left to escort the water cans back to the rear and await their courts-martial.

It was real nice going at first, but then the humps were always nice at the beginning since they were always downhill, to get off the old hill. And it was even a nice day; at least as nice a day as you could want for a hump — fairly cool, since the sun was overcast with what looked like rain clouds. But of course they couldn't be real rain clouds, could they? In the Nam? In May?

When one platoon, the company headquarters section, and half of the next platoon were outside the old perimeter, the column came to its first stop. It was dead quiet so there was no contact and there couldn't be any heat casualties after only thirty minutes. "What the hell's going on?" The word filtered back and a few inched forward to see something.

"It's that battalion radio guy — says he can't make it anymore, won't even try. Griswald's up there beating his ass, and he still says he can't go no farther. There — look at him just laying there taking it."

Lance Corporal Jerry Helman wasn't tired yet, but he was more afraid than he had ever been in his young life — afraid the next three days would be like the first three of this May, afraid he could not push himself through such a time again, and in need of escape from his fear. He was so afraid that he was willing to walk back the same trail to the old perimeter and the water cans and Billings and Lincoln; walk past over two-thirds of the Company, each man every two or three meters starting, glaring, a few envious.

"Couldn't hack it, eh? Have a nice time in the rear, Shithead."

"Thanks for leaving us out here."

"Don't forget to tell your girl back home about this. There, don't cry now."

His war stories back home would always be followed by the worst of qualifications: "Yeah, maybe he done all he said he done but let me tell you — I saw him once quit a hump in the Nam! That's right, he just quit, fell down crying and begging to be sent back — even after some of us beat his ass too. He actually quit on us. We wanted to kill his ass right there!"

Captain Sam sat the Company down where they were and called up his lieutenants. "All right now, you three get this word out once we set in on that objective. This Moy shit is spreading and it's gotta be stopped. These guys ain't tired, they just think they are, and it's your job to see that it don't go no farther. So grab your platoon sergeants and light a fire under them squad leaders. You tell them if anybody pulls this shit again I'm gonna rock them in office hours, and they'll never get promoted in this Company. And tell them I'll decide when they can go on R & R, not whenever they damn well want. Now get back and let's get this moving."

Down off the hill into a dry streambed, between thirty and seventy pounds settled onto each of one hundred twenty-four backs. All but first platoon were now off the old hill and still the lead elements of the column were moving into a gradual downgrade. It felt nice now, but all knew that one of the hated "grunt laws" would soon work its way: "He who humps downhill must sooner or later hump uphill, Man." Patches of shade from the clouds above moved across the ground, giving seconds of relief from the heat. It was nearing one in the afternoon of May 8; so far the hump had been too pleasant to believe. "Six on the hook, Sir."

"This is Six! Look for some shade to put your people under. We gotta stop again since some non-hacker broke the column again. I'm gonna find out who it is, so make sure it ain't none of yours. Six out."

Corporal John Jason Rattner was simply "Rat" to all in his family, school, hometown, and all who had known him in the Corps during his eleven months of service. Before he enlisted, his nickname was a simple shortening of the surname, but after he had been in Vietnam for a couple weeks it took on a new meaning. Corporal J.J. had been the Company's premier tunnel rat for the past six months. He was the one who went down in any bunker or tunnel encountered to search for weapons, supplies, or North Vietnamese. No extra pay was offered for the extra danger, so others were glad to see Rat come along and volunteer.

"You know, most guys don't like that part of being a grunt, but I got to like it after I found out I could be good at it. I've only had to kill two guys I found so far — brought thirteen out alive when I was doing it. I think it was cuz I took the fear out of them, I'd just flash my flashlight on my face when I knew there was one there, and I'd smile — real big, like I'd just knocked off a piece, you know — and they'd come right out. I even brought out two at once one time."

In the past two months Rat had been given an extraordinary responsibility by Sam. He was made mortar section leader, a job normally held by an experienced sergeant. Rat soon knew everything about the three squat 60-millimeter mortars and what they could do. He further learned that he was one of those rarities among 20-year-olds, one who could tell belligerent young men of the same age what to do and not be resented for it. His peers did not feel less than masculine in deferring to his lead.

Today Rat was bothered, and he was determined. He was greatly bothered by the scene put on earlier by the radioman, Helman, and he was determined never to show such weakness himself and burden the whole Company, even though he now felt another of those dizzy, shivering spells coming on. Whenever it happened in the two days before, he would just lie down and wait until it stopped. Everything was perfectly normal afterward, so he had not told a corpsman. But now it had started again, just after Helman quit, and it was worse than before. Rat started to stumble, fell forward, and was too weak to get up. One of the mortar crewmen stayed with him, tried to get him going again as the column continued on by. The last thing Rat wanted was to have the Company stop in the middle of a mission because of some failing on his part. But the last man in the column approached and the word had to be passed to hold it up. Rat's temperature was moving over 103° but, "No, dammit, don't tell Six, don't stop them, I can make it. No, I'll carry my own pack, no . . . ."

Sam came back, saw who it was and all knew there would be no office hours following this halt. "Looks like you got malaria. Why the hell didn't you tell somebody about this?"

"I'll be okay, Captain, don't send me back or call in any chopper. I'll make it all right."

Rat was cooled and led to the head of the column, a few men behind the point. If he fell back again there would be plenty of friends to help him along. In the space of only one hour, Bravo Company had seen within their own number the two opposite extremes of reactions to what they were doing this day worlds away from the States, the real World.

Moving again, a few wondered what else could happen this day but most issued the standard: "Back to the same old shit again — I bet this thing turns out to be ten fucking clicks long." Soon a helicopter could be heard. It cautiously touched down on the old position, hesitated, then lifted off with the water cans and those who thought they couldn't make it anymore. The whump-whump of its rotors lingered over the trees and died off as first platoon came off Bravo Hill, Change 37. The Company would soon be whole again, and alone.

"This is Six! Get on the romeo with that other group moving in on your six o'clock and make liaison with them, and make damn sure nobody shoots anybody when you first see each other. We'll be coming to a blue line up here pretty soon and we'll wait for them there."

In the next half-hour something even more unbelievable than Billings, Helman, and Rattner happened — rain! Rain, in the hot part of the day — "never saw this before, no sir." It started, and remained through the rest of the afternoon, as one of those soft spring rains that beats softly on rooftops and puts people to sleep on dry, warm mattresses under dry, warm blankets. It was one of those gentle nostalgic rains one associates with fireplaces and long ago. As the fat drops soaked helmet covers, dripped onto hot salty necks and traced down lean filthy backs, none of the grunts could imagine what they or anyone else had done to deserve such a gift of coolness. Grateful, relieved bodies slumped back, mouths open to the great faucet and drank it all in: "Soak it up, Man, you'll never see this again in the summer!"

First platoon linked up and moved through everyone else to take the point position. Only a football field length ahead the downgrade came to an end at the anticipated blue line. The stream was larger than most encountered, about fifteen feet wide and three feet deep. On its far bank began an upgrade leading to the finger that would take the grunts straight up to Bravo Hill, Change 38. It was a continuous climb of about one mile.

First platoon pushed on and up and found that the rain had made an otter slide of a hill of only routine slope. With a little muscle and considerable verbal accompaniment, a one hundred foot rope was fixed over the steep rise from the streambed, and the grunts spent the rest of the dark afternoon pulling themselves up the muddy slope. Almost the entire column could hear whenever one of their own slipped and slid down ten, twenty, sometimes fifty meters of the incline. For a few minutes there were the sounds that reminded one of kids sliding down a snow-covered hill, but the laughing and joshing died as soon as the grunts could see the trick of it all. The rain was cooling but the energy a glaring sun would have claimed was spent in making every step sure, and then regaining the lost meters, feet, inches. "The green weenie strikes again, eh, Lieutenant?"

The new hill looked like nothing anyone could anticipate. Usually they're either completely virgin, untouched by either side in the war, or they have been cleared, dug up with incoming holes and then trashed up by former occupants. This one had been thoroughly cleared, was badly cratered and chewed but no humans had walked over it yet. The only things related to man that had been here were the bombs of the B-52s and Phantom jets. It was easy digging into dirt pulverized by the five hundred and one thousand pounders that had rained from 30,000 feet, but here again there was a price exacted for a temporary easing of the task. There were no enemy in this night but almost every man, as he lay waiting for sleep, could feel the rain collecting under and soaking toward him. He could feel it washing away a patch supporting his elbow, hip, foot — changing the mold he had learned to scrape in the ground his first week in the bush, the mold his body had come to like and sleep in. Somebody, or something, was determined to get X amount of sweat out of these men, make them feel and thrash against X intensity of discomfort during each day and night. "That Sky Six ain't cutting no husses this week, Man, not one."

The next morning Sam received word that there would have to be another move. The rain had stopped around three in the morning, so now the sun could bore through a clear sky. Today, May 9, would be a test for one of the three rifle platoons in Bravo, not a test with the North Vietnamese, but a test within the Company, a test concerning reputation. Third platoon, called "Third Herd," had been considered, for several months, the weakest in the Company. A grunt in another platoon described the recent history of the Third Herd: "Third used to be the best, but then on Taylor Common they got hit a couple times and turned to instant shit."

The Herd was the least cohesive, exercised poor noise discipline on humps and poor light discipline at night. Whenever the column on the move was broken it was usually because someone in Third fell behind. But, in the past six weeks, the Herd had gotten a new platoon sergeant and a new platoon commander. Lieutenant Carl Andrews and Staff Sergeant Jerry Goodman were certain the platoon's reputation was no longer deserved, but they needed a chance to prove it. For the past week or more Captain Sam had been thinking it was time to see what improvements the new platoon leadership had been able to affect. This day looked like a good one to find out, considering the moderate length of the move and the appearance of the terrain on the map. The decision was conveyed on the lip of a bomb crater while two men squinted into binoculars.

"Think your people can handle point today?"

"Yes, Sir, I think it's time they had a chance at it."

"Okay, you see that flat-top thing with the downed chopper on it? The one we want is two fingers to the right of it and a little closer to us, the one with that lone white tree on it. Go down this finger here and then use your own judgement."

The going was fast and easy through the first three clicks. It was downhill and it just happened that a load of bombs from a B-52 raid had strung out along the direction of march and cleared most of the brush. Sam and the other platoons were more than surprised at the progress thus far. The halfway point of the hump was a dry streambed, reached at ten-thirty in the morning. The grunts were not nearly as tired as usual, either at this time of day or at this point in the move. "Christ, Man, we're really moving out. This might even turn out to be a half decent hump, you know — the kind we want to write home about!" Without a pause the Herd moved into the second and uphill half of the six thousand meter distance. Sergeant Goodman made the day's last rotation of the point squad, passed up two dull machetes, and Corporal Ken Worthington's nine-man squad took off.

"This is Six! You going up that thing yet?"

"That's affirm — all of mine are on it now but it's gonna be one of them long, gradual rising jobs."

"Yeah, well don't let them think they're tired. Keep at it."

Two hundred meters later Worthington hit a stand of bamboo, one of the two or three most difficult types of growth to move through. The stand turned out to be about one hundred meters wide; it was hacked and cursed through at the expense of all noise discipline, all patience, and much endurance. Before the objective could be reached, two more bamboo stands would have to be cut through. The heat was getting worse and the calls from Sam were successively more impatient, demanding.

"This is Six! Now what's the trouble up there, we should be there by now. You better light a fire under them people and get us up there before this heat really gets bad."

The crest of the hill was finally reached, but only after there were no more fresh arms to swing machetes and after the bamboo was found to be reinforced with the tough, thick vines the grunts had not seen since their last Tarzan movie. Once again the hump had exacted its tribute. "Shit, Man, that could have been an enjoyable little hump but it turns out to be another ball-buster."

Compounding the frustration of the day for one-third of Bravo was the fact that third platoon would not even get a "well-done" for their three hours of work, for Sam lost himself in the details of planning artillery support, verifying his location, calling a re-supply chopper and setting the defenses of "Bravo Hill, Change 39."

"Did the Captain say anything, Sir, I mean about us and all?"

"Fuck no, just the usual get your people tied in with first and second, and dig in, and get them in the shade, and let them eat something, but you and I know how good they were today — we were right with them every step."

"Yes, Sir, they did damn good today, damn good."

After an hour's rest the company gunny collected all the C-4 and began blowing a LZ. The last tree to fall was the tallest — the lone, dead, white and branchless spike, the one on which third platoon had guided for three hours. The grunts were grateful for it, had become attached to it, since its prominent whiteness had led them out of the maddening green maze below. But the minute it was reached and clung to, it became a threat — it was now the best aiming stake a North Vietnamese mortarman could hope to find. It had to go.

Preparations were made, but the tree would not so easily acquiesce to its suddenly reversed value. When the charges placed around its smooth white trunk were detonated, the tree seemed determined to take on a last gasp of life and foil the new security needs that dictated its destruction. It didn't fall in the predicted direction, but right across the middle of the planned helicopter landing zone. The tree now added to the grunts' burden of existence: it had to be moved, somehow pushed or rolled or blasted outside the perimeter and down the slope.

"Before we start that we gotta get some squads out on local patrols and have a look around. Leave your machine guns back, just take a radio and a corpsman and search out that finger and draw down there. You know, look for trails, signs of visitors, see if you can't find a water point somewhere. Call me when you get down in that dark green patch there and I'll tell you whether to come back or whatever else."

Forty-five minutes later Sam called back. "This is Six! Bring your people back as fast as you can — battalion says we gotta move — yeah I know, but they're sending Alpha Company up on this one so we gotta move."

The predictable reaction was predictably quick. "Christ, here we go again — I'd like to get the Colonel out here and see how he'd like humping just to be humping, and twice in one day. That's real fine — we clear the fucking hill for somebody else — real fucking fine. I don't know why they didn't just wait till we pushed that fucking tree down the hill — that would have made the day complete."

At least two of these one hundred twenty-two were determined to preserve some measure of choice over their pawn-like fate. The heaviest equipment a grunt has to carry is the 60-millimeter mortar and its ammunition. The mortars are carried by their gunners, but the ammunition is spread-loaded throughout the Company, one round per man. In the hurried confusion of re-packing things unpacked only two hours before, no call to pick up mortar rounds ever came. And the grunts, once again seeing the agony of thirst and pain without relief as a real and close possibility, willingly and silently assumed the mortarmen would carry their own.

"Hey, Grub, you notice they ain't said nothing about no mortar rounds yet?"

"Yeah, I notice. Just go on packing, and when we move out, act like nothing is different — and don't ask anybody about it, goddam don't ask about it!"

It was a short move, six hundred meters, and consisted of only one descent and one ascent. Both were steeper than usual, however, since the two hills were not in the same, but parallel ridgelines; the deep cut between had to be crossed. The grunts came up with thigh muscles burning and lungs heaving. But at last here was a surprise, a victory of sorts: the new hill had been occupied recently so no LZ had to be cleared, no holes dug for the night. The feeling of injustice at having to clear a hill for someone else was somewhat softened. What happened after the packs were dropped only underlined again the idiocy of this day's succession of events. Captain Sam summoned Andrews and Goodman: "Sergeant Herr tells me third platoon didn't carry any mortar rounds over here. What the hell, your people looked real good on the point this morning and then they pull something like this. Well, since they claim they forgot, they can remember by going back and getting the damn things — get it straightened out."

An armed work party from third platoon retraced the steep route and brought back some forty rounds, but only after a hot exchange with some mortarmen.

"Why the fuck we gotta get your shit when you forgot to give them to us back there? You want the fucking things, you go get them."

"Knock it off, Grub, just go get them. We gotta bird coming in with plenty of water."

The re-supply bird deposited the usual bennies plus freshly-baked bread and pickles. Ten minutes after the chopper crew headed back to their base for warm showers and cold beer, merciful darkness ended further exposure of Bravo. Another company had lived through another day of the war, but within ten of the day's hours a part of that company had displayed both a high degree of professionalism and discipline, and a base selfishness. Vietnam today had exposed to hot open scrutiny some human frailties normally secreted. Score for May 9: no gain.

6

Ho's Birthday

Bravo was now on the ridgeline they had walked those first three days in May, but their direction was reversed. Each of the next three daily humps was hot, of course, but each was also fast, since there was no tangled growth to hack through. And each hill was a little shorter than the last, since the grunts were now making their way back toward the seacoast, where it had all begun. There was only one incident to break the routine.

On the second morning, about a third of a mile into the move, Bravo walked through the battalion field headquarters. The grunts' resentment of the rear-echelon and staff pogues was renewed as they saw the pallets of beer and Coke, the career officers and sergeants — the hated lifers — lounging in sun glasses and lawn chairs. "Look at that shit, will you, fucking folding chairs, and can you believe it — some hot dog up on a pallet with his shirt off, actually trying to get a fucking suntan, trying to get the rays!" The grunts were in no condition to imagine inviting onto one's body the rays which were to them a source of daily discomfort, sometimes of agony.

Five hundred meters beyond the pogues and their headquarters, Bravo stopped for the night. There was light enough for one chopper. It brought the usual water, C-rats and mail, and nine morale-raisers — one Navy chaplain and eight brand new grunts fresh out of training in the World, wearing shiny new flak jackets, clean helmet covers and black boots.

The Chaplain could give a little good feeling by listening to anything a guy wanted to say, even about the lifers. The new troopers could give the grunts much more. Handled properly, newbys could be sources of laughter and the feeling of being important, knowledgeable and no longer on the bottom of the hierarchy in the bush. The gunny called the platoon sergeants and assigned each of the newcomers. They were taken back to each platoon commander for their first word on what really goes on in the Nam.

"Now, we don't want to see no John Wayne performances out here. Just do your job and listen to your fire team and squad leaders — they're the ones who'll teach you everything and help you get through the next few months."

The veteran grunts listened hard, small smiles growing across their faces. They couldn't wait to get their hands on one of these scared young bodies; if they could spare the moisture they would probably be drooling. They were hungry to repeat the words each of them had cringed under months or weeks before: "Hey, new guy, let me show you how to do that there," and at night on the lines, "Now you hear that? That ain't a gook, it's probably a rock ape or maybe a tiger, and if you ever think . . . ."

"Hold it! You mean there's tigers and gorillas over here?"

"Oh, hell yes — see them all the time — sometimes they come right up to the line at night and attack guys, but not every night, not every night."

The next morning battalion called to report that Bravo would stay on their present hill for several days. So patrol routes were planned, foxholes and ammunition bunkers were dug, fields of fire were cleared. Four hours later, battalion called back, this time directing Sam to be ready to move his Company in one hour. Sam didn't like the word change, nor did his grunts but "this looks like real good hunting around here." "Well fuck, here we go again, digging holes for somebody else again — for nothing."

The move was delayed when the chopper coming for the water cans, outgoing mail and the Chaplain drew fire from the next ridgeline to the north. The green tracers didn't come very close to the bird but they were close enough to call an air strike. Two Phantom jets were circling overhead in ten minutes. The grunts let out a chorus of "oo — get some, Sweetheart!" as each load of bombs exploded against the suspected hillside, but the North Vietnamese answered with new bursts of fire between sorties. The Phantom pilots then switched to napalm, and Sam added artillery to the air attack; the enemy gun was finally silent.

Though the threat was soon ended, the grunts were reminded that there was an enemy out there even though he had not shown himself recently. Once begun, it was a fast move. It proved a shock to the newbys when the heat exhaustion claimed one. Third platoon was on point and saw the chance to work something on the rest of the Company that would kill forever their bad reputation. "They're all the time saying we're the ones that break the column. Well fuck them, this time they can try and keep up with us." So the Third Herd took off, faster than they might have, had they known just where the break in the column would occur. Company commanders don't like to get lost or to have to slow down their platoons on their own account, but the predictable bitch sounded sweet coming from someone else for a change.

"This is Six! Dammit all, you had better slow that outfit down and send somebody back to link up with my radioman!"

At Sam's meeting with platoon leaders that night, nothing was said of the embarrassing break in the column caused by third platoon's racehorse tactics. There was much heavier news to consider. Sam reported that just after Bravo left its position, Delta Company had moved onto the same hill and immediately received twenty-seven rounds of incoming. "That's what those choppers are for over there, taking out their wounded." It was the third time in five days that Delta had been hit after occupying a position vacated the same day by another company. Both previous times, the departing unit had received no incoming, no enemy contact during its tenure on the positions. The North Vietnamese seemed to prefer certain Americans over others as targets.

Things had been going smoothly for Bravo long enough now — three days. And there was another reason for a few to sense it might be time for another day of idiocy: the day was the thirteenth of the month. At eight in the morning all of third platoon headed out to set up an L-shaped ambush at the junction of two streams, some 300 meters outside the company perimeter. Four hours later first platoon was to move into one of the streambeds leading to the ambush site and push slowly toward third platoon, nudging the North Vietnamese in the area into the ambush ahead. If no enemy were flushed, first platoon was to assume the same ambush site as third returned to the Company base. Third platoon's ambush was conducted with no enemy appearing. On his way back up the hill to the Company area, Lieutenant Andrews stopped to watch first move into the site. Seeing the point squad move on through the stream junction, Andrews called the first platoon commander, George Sorenson.

"One actual, this is Three! Be informed your point is past the promised land, over."

"Roger that, Three. I'm gonna have a look around, see if I can't find a better one, over."

Andrews turned and put third back on the move upward. Twenty minutes later a burst of gunfire from the ambush sight froze the column, turned all eyes back and downward. First platoon had not only moved past the ambush site but without realizing it, outside the battalion area of operation as well. Then, as he rounded a sharp bend in the stream, Sorenson's point man almost bumped into three North Vietnamese loaded down with rice and ammunition. The three NVA scrambled up out of the stream and took off across the flat grassy flood plain for the nearest hill as the first five men in the column opened up. One of the three was hit but all got away. Sam was on the radio while the gunfire was still echoing through the draws, over the grass.

"Is that your people, Three?"

"That's a negative! It's One, over."

"You know where he's at?"

"He's around six or seven hundred meters past my old promised land, over."

"What the hell's he doing out there, that's outa the damn AO! Get off a minute, I want him on the line."

"Six, this is One, go."

"You know where you're at? You got anybody hurt down there? How the hell'd you miss it by five hundred or whatever? Well, you get that outfit together and stay where you are, we got some air coming in."

So first platoon, eager to pursue the three "visitors" and bring something back to Sam to atone for their map-reading error, stayed low against the stream bank and just waited. Within five minutes a "Bronco," a twin engine observation plane, was circling overhead. The aerial observer was eager too, and let loose too soon with a burst of .50 caliber rounds. Huddled against the stream bank below, Lance Corporal Paul Stanton turned to see who had just stepped on his shoulder. Instead of someone standing next to him, he saw the fiberglass plates falling out of the left shoulder of his flak jacket, and then, blood coursing onto the dirt. "Hey, Lieutenant, that fucking cowboy upstairs got Stanton in the shoulder!" The "cowboy" made a few more passes, slamming half a dozen rockets into a hillside before he was called off. A medevac chopper was called and in fifteen minutes Stanton was on his way out of the bush. Now first platoon could start back home.

It had retraced only about 300 meters of the route in the streambed when there was another casualty. Private Garth Corley had felt lousy all night and on the way out to the ambush in the morning. And he felt lousy after yesterday's fast hump; it was his first, since he was one of the newbys. His body was only beginning to acclimatize; he had gone as far as he could and now collapsed in the stream. He was hot, dry and flushed when the corpsman got to him.

Corley was stripped and laid in the water as an intravenous solution was injected into his arm. He was carried a few yards, then put back in the water, carried a distance, then dunked again until they reached the last area suitable for an evacuation by helicopter before the trail wound up the hill — a bomb crater. The chopper pilot could not touch down on the crater's edge without putting the rotors into a tree so he hovered twenty feet above and lowered a cable and harness from a side hatch. With the rotors raising a blinding, stinging cloud of the loose dirt in the crater, three grunts strapped Corley to the cable and signaled the crew chief to take him up. In the swirling chaos in the crater the harness had been placed on Corley upside-down so he now dangled by his legs, still unconscious. Carefully lowered, he was rigged and taken up, finally on his way to an alcohol bath in the air-conditioned wards at Quang Tri. At last, first platoon could begin the long climb home.

The blunders, trials and missed chances of the day were set aside in the exhilaration over what the re-supply chopper had brought — carrots, cucumbers, tomatoes, C-rats, new socks and jungle uniforms, orange juice, grape juice, mail, water, and 300 mortar rounds, many more than the Company could carry. "Hey, B.J., you see them boxes off to the side? Mortar rounds, hundreds of them. That means we stay for awhile, Man!"

As night and the fog came down, the mortar gunners fired one hundred rounds out around the perimeter, half of them in the open area where first platoon had found the three NVA. Every half hour through the night they would fire three or four rounds to discourage any approach to their hill. Alpha, Charlie, and Delta companies were doing the same thing, for all were set for a few days now. At eleven-thirty the 81-millimeter mortar section of battalion headquarters sent two rounds toward a hill they were certain was unoccupied by Americans.

One of the fat green missiles exploded fifty meters outside the machine gun position of Corporal Manuel Rodriguez, the same Rodriguez who had been fired at by Dennis Moy nine days before. The second round landed twenty meters from the sleeping areas of Andrews and Goodman. Except for a temporary hearing loss in the three, there were no injuries. This time, Rodriguez had company as he wondered, "Why?" The next morning George Sorenson wrote his bride of eight months that he had just played a major role in a day that would never make it in the official Defense Department histories.

Captain Sam didn't sleep well that night, not because battalion had fired at him but because the day was so full of missed opportunities. How could an entire platoon wander six hundred meters out of its assigned area — don't they train these kids anymore? And how, when they found three NVA too loaded down to even fire back, could they help but bring back three bodies? The Company needed to see some bodies, needed to see what all the humping over the endless string of hills was all about. Maybe if battalion would extend the area of operation Bravo could work the area and come up with something? Battalion returned the call at six the next morning: Bravo could work the area but only for one day; they would be moving out the following morning.

May fourteenth dawned bright and clear. Fog was burned out of the draws and streambeds by six-thirty. Today Sam was taking out two of his three platoons, second and third, all of his six machine guns and one of the three mortars. In the training manuals this would be called a Company-minus patrol. First platoon would rest today and take the point tomorrow. By seven-thirty the Company-minus was down off the hill and in yesterday's ambush sight. The two platoons spread out on either side of the stream, up the low foothills and fingers, and slowly swept toward the area of first platoon's encounter.

"This is Six! Send some people up each of these here draws and streambeds as you come to them — that's where the little people hide their goodies. Take your time, we got all day." Everything went smoothly, quietly, until about eight-thirty when Doc Richards told Andrews he had a heat casualty. "What do you mean a heat casualty, it ain't even nine o'clock yet!"

"Temperature of a hundred and four. You better take a look at him, over here in the stream. I noticed he looked real weak after we got off the hill, then a little later he just fell over in the water."

PFC Delmar Stowe was a recruiter's dream — six feet four, two hundred fifteen pounds when he was sent from his home in Philadelphia to boot camp at Parris Island, South Carolina. Most important, Stowe wanted to join, just like his two older brothers had wanted it when they were eighteen. Doc Richards suspected what had overcome Stowe was more serious than the usual heat exhaustion, but he was not at all prepared for the truth. "You're a what? How did you ever get through boot camp? Why did you come in the green machine when you had the perfect deferment?"

"Both my older brothers was in so I wanted to join, and all my friends was in the Marines or Army and I didn't want to stay home when everyone else was over here. First I tried the Army, but they said they don't take anybody who's had diabetes, but the Marines said they'd take me." A three-man security detail was left with Stowe. He would be picked up when the two platoons headed back to the hill for the night.

The grunts slowly worked down the stream some eight or nine hundred meters, examining every fold in the terrain. Only a few footprints, a pair of North Vietnamese tennis shoes and a fuselage section from a shot-down helicopter were found. Sam turned the patrol around and headed for home. No NVA bodies, no blood trails, no rice, no mortar rounds. Half way up the hill the Company experienced its second casualty of a quiet day. With the carrots and clean socks, yesterday's re-supply bird had brought another new guy, this one a new lieutenant fresh from training.

Second Lieutenant Tom Henderson, like PFC Stowe, wanted the Marine Corps program and he wanted some time in the Nam with a line company. He was getting a quick introduction. At his arrival Sam told him he would be going on every patrol with every platoon for the next few days, "so you'll know what goes on out here, and to get yourself acclimatized and all." Henderson made it through the patrol all right but the climb back got him. One of the corpsmen had him under a bush beside the main trail. Over half the Company filed by and saw him on his back, pale and gasping. It was not the best way to be introduced to those whose performance and safety he would soon be charged with.

"Hey, you see that new second looey?"

"Yeah, a real humper, eh? I'd like to know where they get some of them non-hackers and then I'd like to know how they ever get through that OCS. Must not be nothing like boot camp, you know?"

"Yeah, must be a real skate."

Attachments to this hill had been formed, most with good reason according to the value system of the grunt. It did not have to be cleared of any tangled growth and someone else had dug all the incoming holes. No one was real excited about leaving the next morning — not because they had to start at five in the morning, not because leaving meant another hump, but because they were leaving a place that had offered some relief from the monotony of walking under the heat and a pack, of digging holes and being tired and pissed off all the time. From this hill the grunts had at least seen some NVA — there really was a live enemy out there somewhere. But even that small regret was soon forgotten as the grunts got down into the valley they had swept the day before. More than a few looked back in relief, a measure of victory. They had made it — the merciless humps were over. Surely nothing in the future could duplicate that exhaustion, that madness of moving just to be moving for fifteen days. Now they were down off the last one, the easternmost hill in Virginia Ridge. Now they would be moving where breezes flow close to the ground, in the flat grassy plain that becomes beach on the South China Sea. "Hey, can you believe this shit? It's flat, Man — like a fucking airport!"

The one-mile move turned out to be the nicest hump of the operation, one even bordering on the enjoyable. A cloud cover shielded Bravo from the sun, and as they walked past the last checkpoint and turned toward the ocean, a small breeze came up. Faces lifted, flak jackets were held

106

open to receive as much of the miracle as possible before it was taken away and the heat came back. "Oh Man, that old Sky Six is really coming through, ain't he?" Both the cloud cover and the breeze held until the objective was reached. And what an objective — so low it could barely be distinguished from the other small undulations on the horizon. At its base the grunts were saying things they could only dream of saying in the previous two weeks, for this "hill" was only 125 meters above sea level, not 289, not 367. "You heard it Man, the Lieutenant says this thing's a hundred twenty-five meters high. This ain't no hill, Man, it's a fucking pimple! I don't know if I can make it, it's gonna be a real ass-kicker — ha!"

The grunts were into the flatlands, determined to skate. Coming out of two weeks of endless humping through superheated hills, they felt justified in their determination. They thus deliberately ignored a law of life in the bush they had all seen proved: the jungle, the hills, the sun, the war exact X amount of patience or sweat or blood from all who live closest to the workings of those forces. For the most part, the grunts got away with their skating. But not one of them could possibly have guessed what a crazy mix of blunders, near-misses and the unnecessary would fill Bravo's time in the flatlands.

For one, there was the night "the Hunter" came over the radio. "This is the Hunter! Bravo Six will die tonight. All yankee devils will die tonight. Don't fall asleep, American." Sam put the Company on full alert before answering the challenge. "Come on out, Hunter, let's have it out tonight."

"Brave Bravo Six will die tonight. Do not sleep tonight."

"Yeah, you sound good on the radio — we'll see you guys in Hanoi next week."

"Americans sleep forever after tonight. Watch for the Hunter tonight."

For forty-five minutes the grunts wondered out loud whether the Hunter was a North Vietnamese who had mastered English or the soldier they had all heard about, the tall blonde American who had defected and was advising the NVA in the field. The Hunter turned out to be neither. He was Gunnery Sergeant Harold Zell and he was calling from an American tank base ten miles to the east. After a few beers in the club, Zell felt the need for a little excitement, so he climbed into one of his tanks and turned the radio dials until he stumbled onto a field unit's frequency. Gunny Zell then spread as much terror as the listening unit could work up in its collective imagination.

And, there was the night Private First Class Paul Jenkins showed more carelessness than usual. Jenkins was known for losing things, misplacing things, forgetting things and for leaving his pistol and grenade launcher on "fire" when they should be on "safe." One night Jenkins fell asleep holding his pistol. Something caused his trigger finger to contract and Jenkins' forty-five sent a bullet whistling through the night air. But before it lifted into the cool breeze off the sea, the bullet disturbed the quiet air two inches above the right ear of Corporal Roger DeHaan, Jenkins' squad leader. Jenkins was later fined twenty-five dollars by his company commander.

Then there was the day Sam conferred his approval on the Third Herd. Andrews' platoon had taken point on one of the daily moves and had done well. After the Company was settled, Sam called a meeting with the Herd's squad leaders. He told them they had made much improvement in the past few weeks and he no longer considered them the weakest platoon in the Company. Those who had been with Sam more than a few weeks now wondered if he had been affected by the heat, for nearly everyone knew he offered compliments about as frequently as he expressed laughter — very rarely. Sam knew he was considered excessively critical, demanding, more like a machine than a human, but he also knew that to preserve every grunt's chances for a safe return to the States he had to constantly push people to produce what they considered impossible or unnecessary. He had to be sparing in his praise to keep his grunts tough. After meeting with their commander, the grunts went back to wondering how much more of the unexpected the operation held.

While Sam was grudgingly admired for several of his abilities, he was detested for others. Those for which he was detested were related to the fact that he intended to make a career of the military — Sam was a lifer. He was also a proud and sensitive combat leader. Sam was proud of the fact that he had never gotten his company lost in the jungle or in the hills, he had never left anything useful to the enemy at a former position or along the trail, and he had the highest body count in the battalion. Now on the latest operation Sam was sensitive of a certain development, one which did nothing to uphold his reputation: the other companies in the battalion had more enemy contacts than Bravo so far. All Bravo had produced lately were heat casualties. Another career-oriented individual

108

in the battalion thought he saw in this situation the chance to engage in the game of one-upmanship that would enhance his own career pattern.

A few hours after Bravo left Hill 125, Alpha Company assumed the position, and the company commander decided he had found some equipment left behind by Bravo. He was only too willing to report his find. The next morning, battalion called Sam on the matter. The operations officer was professionally tactful in passing on the veiled admonition, "See if you can't do something about this kind of thing in the future, cuz you know how hot the Old Man is on hanging onto your gear." No company commander could stand for the implication that his troops were so poorly disciplined as to intentionally discard essential gear. Sam called a meeting of all his staff NCOs and officers and explained the situation. "That fucking Alpha Six — we can't take an accusation like that and do nothing about it!" The discussion of what to do lasted well after sunset.

Finally, wrapped up in what he thought to be the ultimate loyalty, the executive officer volunteered to take a detail back to 125 and check out the allegation. Now the only question was who would accompany the exec on the mission. Sam made it sound like an open question, but he knew his grunts were far too precious to risk on so selfish a mission, so it was to the honor and pride of his career sergeants that he appealed in describing the necessity of the detail. With visions of fitness reports subtly dangled before their eyes, the three staff sergeants "volunteered." The patrol, certainly one of the least sensible ever run by an American force in the entire war, left the perimeter at seven the next morning.

An hour later, Alpha Company called, reporting that there had been some confusion, the man who found the gear was mistaken, the matter wasn't really important and should be dropped. So, halfway to Hill 125 the patrol was called back. On this day the troops saw demonstrated the special vanities of which lifers are capable. There was no longer any room for doubt in young minds now. To the junior officers and grunts who talked about it for days after, the special patrol provided just "another reason why" — another reason not to stay in the Corps beyond the first enlistment.

And then there was the most memorable day of all in the flatlands, the day Bravo Company observed Ho Chi Minh's birthday. On May 19, 1969, the leader of the Vietnamese nationalist movement and of the Democratic Republic of Vietnam would be seventy-nine years old. It was widely known that communist forces had a habit of launching major attacks on national holidays or birthdays of historical figures, so Sam asked for some reinforcement from the eighteenth to the twenty-first. Since Bravo was in an area flat enough to support several roads, the grunts were augmented by two tanks. For the day preceding Ho's birthday, Sam planned a complete perimeter sweep to make sure no NVA would crawl up to an attack position. What he had in mind for second and third platoons was a coordinated patrol, a sweeping-force, blocking-force action like the ambush-turned-fiasco first and third had run a week before. Sam figured it was impossible for either unit to get lost this time, since there were both roads and streams in the area. The plan was simple: the platoons would leave the perimeter in opposite directions; second, and one of the tanks, would ambush a road-stream junction; third would sweep down a streambed toward second. If no enemy were pushed into the ambush, the platoons would go back home by different routes, at different times.

Three hours after it began, the patrol took on the potential for disaster. With no enemy sighted and only 100 meters remaining between the ambush and third platoon in the streambed, the coordinated phase of the patrol was over. Each unit began to change course and move into its assigned route home. The third platoon point man, PFC Ron Tobias, was the first man out of the stream; he looked ahead and froze. He was the first in either platoon to realize the tank crew had not received word about his unit's whereabouts — they were still looking for the NVA to shoot. Tobias watched as the tank's barrel swung toward him, stopped and lowered to his height. He looked down the deep, dark 90-millimeter gun tube seventy-five meters away for about half a second, then dove head-first down the ten-foot embankment. Then came the ear splitting wham and a screaming whoosh as two hundred quarter-inch ball bearings from the tank's anti-personnel round flew a few feet overhead. Andrews grabbed the radio, "Bravo! Bravo! Bravo! This is Three! Get that bull off us, over!" Again the wham and whoosh overhead. And a tree across the stream disappeared. "Bravo! Bravo! This is Three! He's still after us — get him off, get him off!"

The tank was finally reached and silenced, but the driver was sure he saw some NVA instead of friendlies, so second platoon turned around and swept along the west embankment as third sat and waited on the east. No NVA bodies. Ron Tobias and the rest of third platoon decided to take a break. "Fucking tankers can't even tell the difference between us and gooners — guess people get stupid as hell when they ride everywhere they go instead of humping."

Two hours after the American tank fired at the American grunts, the latter were walking into their Company perimeter. They could see a definite improvement in the patrol base — on the landing zone sat a pallet of beer. They could also see that no one seemed to notice their return. There was a crowd around a tank that had moved inside the perimeter to assume a night defensive position. Rolling past the mortar pits, it had set off a mine. The tank had its right tread blown off; Bravo had five mortarmen injured. It was not a fragmentation mine so the injuries were broken legs, rocks and dirt driven under the skin, and temporary deafness instead of punctured lungs and intestines, and severed limbs. All of the five would return. For the next two hours, while the ice around the beer melted and drew a dark red line down the tank trail, the grunts probed with knives at the dry hard earth for more booby traps. Three details of a dozen men each crawled on hands and knees, shoulder to shoulder. Their cautious jabbing uncovered five more of the large flat Russian mines.

In the final hour of daylight the beer was distributed. No one could tell it had once been cold. Far to the north in Hanoi, Uncle Ho would be most pleased to know what his birthday had meant to one American company.

The next morning the futility of tanks in Vietnam was further illustrated. A tank with a towbar arrived and began dragging the disabled tank back to its base. The rescue vehicle got only one hundred meters down the road before losing a tread of its own on yet another mine. The grunts could find no sympathy for the crews of the two crippled tanks.

"Now ain't that too bad — them tankers will have to do a little walking for their showers and beer tonight!"

"Yeah, and carry their own Cokes and all them Cs, tough shit, eh?"

Only one occurrence during the days in the flatlands contributed to the accomplishment of Bravo Company's mission. One afternoon a squad from second platoon found a cache of fifty-two 82-millimeter rounds and fuses for North Vietnamese mortars. The cache was one of thousands like it placed all over South Vietnam. Viet Cong and North Vietnamese attacks are planned around the locations of such deposits of food and ammunition. The mortar rounds were discovered when Lance Corporal Archie Lawson almost tripped the booby trap wire that would have detonated the entire cache and taken his squad with it. Lawson's squad returned the following day and blew the cache with demolition charges.

The rest of Bravo Company's time in the flatlands was filled by just about all the small hour-by-hour activities experienced by all other grunts in all other wars. There were 27 poker games played, 137 weapons cleaned, seven mustaches grown, six night ambushes run, 328 foxholes and 12 mortar pits dug, an uncountable number of bitches uttered, two promotions awarded, 488 malaria pills taken, 1220 C-ration meals eaten, 125 cans of Seven-Up drunk, 389 pieces of mail (which included one birth announcement and three Dear Johns) received, 93 canteens of Kool-Aid mixed, 18 guards caught sleeping on post ("Must be a bad battery in the radio, Captain"), nine cases of diarrhea suffered, 347 letters written, and an infinite number of sexual conquests dreamed.

7

Moaning and Groaning

Operation Virginia Ridge was now twenty days old. It was not only unusual for a rifle company in a combat zone to walk almost three weeks and encounter no ambushes, no firefights, it was unheard of. The quiet had of course been welcome, but by now all the grunts were nervous about it. It couldn't last forever, could it? Uncle Ho up in Hanoi wasn't about to give it all up now, was he? As all knew it would, the word to move out again came. This time it provoked, not the usual bitches, but a slightly ominous quiet. The word was that the grunts would be moving toward the north for the next few days.

The rest of Virginia Ridge turned out to be a steady movement toward the Demilitarized Zone, the five-mile-wide strip that had divided Vietnam since the Geneva Convention of 1954. Throughout its existence, the DMZ has come to mean different things to different people. To the diplomats who drew it, the line represented a face-saving truce to a problem whose solution was too deeply tied up with personal vanity and national honor to be dealt with realistically, a truce which saved but little western face and few Vietnamese lives. To the Vietnamese living south of it, the line meant a flimsy guarantee that rice could be planted and harvested in peace, that a governing group could have its sovereignty recognized the world over. To the Vietnamese living north of it, the line was a constant and humiliating reminder that the reunification of a homeland and a way of life, ravaged by westerners for more than a century, was still unfinished.

To the young grunts who would walk toward it now, the DMZ meant other things still, some things known and some not. In the first place, the Z was the reason the grunts were in Vietnam; if it had never been violated, the grunts could be making decent money, chasing girls, fixing up their cars, getting drunk or going to school back in the World. For now, walking toward the Z meant walking back up on Virginia Ridge and that, of course, meant humping the hills again. It also meant there would be a slight increase in danger, since everyone knew there were NVA north of the line, while south of it there were, between encounters with those same NVA, days of boredom and safety. The rest of what moving to the Z meant was not known by anyone, not Sam, not the general, not the most daring of diviners.

The tanks and grunts both moved out at six in the morning, the former rumbling back home to the east, the latter cursing and farting off to the north. After 800 meters Bravo stopped so Sam could examine the terrain ahead through field glasses and talk on the radio with Charlie Company. The two companies were to meet on Charlie's position of the night before, then Bravo would push on for some 1400 meters and a one-night stand.

At their link-up an hour later, the grunts of Charlie were relieved to see friendly faces again. All they had seen the previous two nights were North Vietnamese faces. A platoon of NVA hit Charlie's lines three times in those two nights, and followed each assault with mortar barrages through the remainder of the night. The score so far was twelve NVA dead to four dead Americans. The scene on top of Charlie's hill was anything but a model of tactical discipline. It was a mob scene, as the latest and friendly visitors crowded around the grunts of Charlie to hear about the last two nights.

"Did they come right up to your lines?" —

114

"How many was there?" —

"How many confirms you get?" —

"Did they have rockets?" —

"Did they use gas on you?"

Bravo was up and on the move again in fifteen minutes, just as the heat was starting to get up. The map showed a streambed about seven hundred meters ahead, and there Sam expected to find a temporary NVA patrol base. "Second, you take point and pick your point man real careful — there's gotta be something a little ways ahead." Six hundred meters ahead the Company heard two shots. Safety selectors clicked off down the column; against the silence born of fear, they seemed as loud as freight car couplings taking up slack. The column dropped to the ground. "Hey, that don't sound like a 16 or a 47 . . . and only two of them. What the shit?"

The two rounds had come from Lieutenant Herb Marriott's pistol, and they had killed two North Vietnamese regulars. Second platoon had been careful enough to sneak up on a small bunker complex on the stream without being seen or heard. The point man began hearing voices, halted the Company, and signaled for Marriott. The two advanced slowly toward the voices — "They sound like a bunch of damn turkeys, them gooks, you know, gobble, gobble" — the rest of the second platoon inching along behind. The trail went into a small bend, straightened and, "There we were, me and my radioman and two gooks, just staring at each other. They had this dumb look on their faces — I guess we did too — like, how you guys get here, you know?" Marriott was the only one of the four to speak: "Lai dai, lai dai" (come here, come here).

The two NVA looked at each other and ran for the nearest bunker. Marriott fired two shots from about twenty feet and the two enemy fell dead on top of their bunker. Such shooting was not typical of the average marine, but the result was no less final for its luck. Resuming the hump, the grunts filed by the fresh bunkers and saw their first dead NVA in two months. All the newbys acquired by the Company in two months came up with the predictable reaction. "Jeez, I heard they were small but not that small. That one looks like he's about twelve years old. Jeez!"

The last eight hundred meters of the hump produced six more heat casualties. Canteens were filled in the stream and Sam decided enough daylight remained for a break in the shade. Fifteen minutes later first platoon began trailing out toward the objective but had to stop when two

115

more heat casualties developed. Another break in the shade was ordered. For the remainder of the move the grunts walked a hundred meters, laid in the shade for ten minutes, then walked another hundred meters. Even the old salts and short-timers thought it was unusually hot. "Christ, I can't remember it getting this hot, can you?" An unexpected stream, not on the map, was found and fallen into. The grunts poured helmetsful over their heads, down shirts and pants, then moved on, back to another of the humps that had to be completed.

Just before the second stream was found, Lance Corporal Thomas Ecroyd's mind decided it was time to reverse the madness of the hump and the heat. It was time to say screw it, time to survive. Ecroyd tripped on a tree root and rolled downhill into the man ahead. When his buddies tried to help him back up he started moaning and his legs refused to support any weight or take another step. His pack, rifle and canteens were carried by others and he was half pushed, half carried the remaining distance.

"Six, this is Three. Be informed I got four heat casualties but am not stopped. We'll bring them in but we might break the column."

"This is Six! Leave a squad back with them who think they're so thirsty and keep the other two squads on the column, then when you get up here I want the names of them non-hackers."

Just after the last man in the Company reached the objective, Ecroyd's protest took a violent and directed turn. At the sight of Sam, Ecroyd began running up the hill screaming, "I'm gonna kill you, you bastard! Leave us alone! You want to kill us, all of us — I'm gonna kill you, kill you, kill you . . . ." He fell, clawing the earth, his face reflecting more exhaustion and disillusion than his mind could contain.

Sam's verdict was characteristic. "These non-hacking babies get every damn thing they want growing up back in the States, then they get over here in a war and they think they get a little tired, they just think they're so tired. Hell, he could go another five clicks today at least. He just thought he was through."

Ecroyd was sent out on the next chopper for his psychiatric evaluation. The grunts debated into the next day whether Ecroyd had staged a scene like the Dennis Moy incident of two and a half weeks before just to get out of the bush, or whether he really had, like Moy, cracked in the heat. They decided it probably was the real thing when they learned later they

116

had humped through a 118° afternoon.

On the other side of the hill Herb Marriott debated something else in his mind: how had five hours of practice in firing the pistol on the training range prepared him to shoot with the perfection he had shown today? That night the grunts rested on soil 3500 meters from the DMZ.

The next morning all of Bravo but one platoon moved out to the north. Second would make the move after sending out the water cans. The hump was short and it was over before the heat had a chance to do any damage, but it ended in a climb sharp enough to break a free-running sweat on one hundred twenty-six bodies. It turned out to be one of those rare enjoyable moves. The grunts could smile and laugh as they bargained over the meager treat they deserved.

"If you get a heat tab and the rest of the makings, I'll put in the water for coffee."

"Thought you'd never ask, Miss — do it for us and this time put in four sugars."

The grunts were told in the morning where they were — two thousand meters south of the DMZ — but it didn't mean much to most. Their hump for the day was already over. But being 2000 meters away from the Z meant a lot to Sam and his plans for the safety of Bravo. It meant that Bravo was just within range of the North Vietnamese 61-millimeter, and well within that of enemy 82-millimeter mortars and all sizes of rockets. Later in the afternoon, however, the idea of 2000 meters took on more meaning to each of the other lives here on the new position, Hill 130. Two choppers arrived with two 81-millimeter mortars and their crews.

"Hey, Chief, you see what the birds brought?"

"Yeah, no mail and two 81s."

"Wonder why; think we're gonna stay awhile?"

"That ain't what the Lieutenant said. He says we're gonna keep humping it toward the Z, but shit, who knows? Don't sweat it though, you won't be humping them 81s."

Sam held up sundown until his new and bigger mortars were dug in. Two squads from first platoon and one from second would have the ambushes this first night on 130; third and the rest would have the perimeter watch. One of the ambushes would be on the stream touching the western slope of the new position. The other would be farther down the same stream. Both were set half an hour after sunset. Five hours later the shadows began to move for Lieutenant George Sorenson and his squads on ambush.

A night in the Nam always comes alive to some degree — things are either seen or heard. If something is both seen and heard, it usually turns out to be a tiger, rock ape or North Vietnamese. With a half-moon out tonight Sorenson expected to see bushes move and work on the imagination. This time he and his grunts also began hearing whatever it was out there, and the small noises were coming closer. A few moments later sounds and human forms came together. The suspected NVA re-supply trail turned out to be exactly that. A small shock set in — battalion intelligence was actually right for once. Then a larger shock — there were more than a handful of NVA in this party. One grunt measured the number of enemy as "a whole shitpot full!" Sorenson got on the radio and whispered his discovery back to Sam. "Six, this is One. I think I got some visitors out here."

"This is Six, keep your people alert out there and let me know what happens. Don't let them get excited — it could be some damn rock apes, you know." Sam had received dozens of such calls during his tour and since he knew what the night could do to a tired and scared grunt's perceptions, he greeted all with skepticism.

In as little time as it took him to press the transmission button on his radio, Sorenson was back. "This is One. I can see them now, there's about seven or eight moving right for us, all in a row."

"Okay now, let their point go on by, and hit their middle, then we'll wipe up the ends after."

But this was no small reconnaissance in a local area. "Six, this is One. I'm still counting and twenty-seven have gone past us so far — some are really loaded down looks like. They just keep coming!" Sorenson had never seen anything like it but Sam recognized it as a major re-supply movement. The NVA were going to plant some new ammunition and food caches in the area. Within a month an infantry unit would follow and use the supplies to support operations against the Americans and South Vietnamese here in Quang Tri Province.

Sam put the Company perimeter on 100 percent alert and told the mortar crews to get all the ammo they could find ready by the tubes. Then back to Sorenson. "Can you tell how many of them there is yet?"

118

"They're still coming — there's thirty-nine, forty, forty-one, forty-two . . . ."

Sensing that he was on the verge of a beautiful body count, his first in months, Sam could barely control himself as he told his lieutenant what would happen next. "Now listen, you're gonna get six rounds of HE right on them, then the illumination will start. You open up as soon as the first six rounds hit them, not before, or you're liable to get yourself overrun in the dark. Then you stay there and move the 60s around on them after they start to split up and scatter — and don't let your men chase anybody, stay there."

Before the privates and corporals took over for the evening Sam had one last message for the mortar crews. "This is Six! Now don't mess it up, it's gonna be six HE, then the illum. Get them rounds right next to you with the safety wires off, One actual's gonna tell you when. When I hear them first rounds splash, I want to hear a lotta fire and a lotta gooks screaming. I better see nothing but heads and arms and legs flying — and don't let any of them get away to tell about it!"

Four seconds later Sorenson whispered "fire" to the gun pits. Over one hundred North Vietnamese ammunition and rice-bearers froze as they heard those six rounds, fat with death and pain, leave their tubes in quick succession — thunk-thunk-thunk. The enemy column did about all it could do — walk a little faster and hope the shells were meant for someone else. But fourteen seconds later, as the rounds quietly whistled back to earth through the cool air, they knew they were to be the victims tonight. The first rounds overshot the column, but they were close enough to stop all thought in North Vietnamese heads about empty stomachs, girl friends, sore feet or reuniting the fatherland.

After Sorenson called back an aiming adjustment, at least half of each volley hit within twenty-five meters of the trail. The North Vietnamese were seeing and hearing explosions in front of them and behind them — blinding white flashes, massive rushes of wind and thousands of white-hot steel fragments were shattering young bodies, shattering myths about what poor matches the imperialistic American aggressors were for the battalions of Uncle Ho and General Giap. Then the crack and rattle of M-16s and machine guns at close range filled the night.

The grunts were only about fifty feet away from the enemy trail — it was difficult to miss, even in the dark. The ambushing rifles and machine guns built their fire to a crescendo, held it for a few seconds, then slowed as each man and crew picked an individual target. Sam just listened and stared at where the red tracer bullets and mortar explosions blipped and streaked through the darkness. He wasn't happy, he was ecstatic. And, at the karump-rump-rump of each volley of mortar rounds splashing, at each burst of rifle fire, the grunts back on the perimeter looked at each other and grinned — "Get some, Man, oh get some! Shit, why can't I be down there!"

Sam interrupted his spectating long enough to call an artillery battery. He wanted to saturate the area around the ambush and pick up any enemy scattering back to the north. In fifteen minutes a twin-engine spotting plane was overhead and the 155-millimeter rounds were whistling in from the Army battery four miles away at Con Thien. With the spotting plane came the large support plane, Puff the Magic Dragon. Through the night Puff droned high overhead in a tight circle, dropping basketball flares and spraying the area with his guns. "Get some, Big Man, get some!"

Sam and the Defense Department's technology were turning this once lush and life-giving land into a surrealistic stage suggesting the place where one awakes after his funeral. Shadows were pushed across the yellow-orange ground and brush by flares falling slowly on tiny parachutes, swells of red light came out from behind trees and draws as each artillery barrage impacted, and Puff's tracer bullets stitched a gently waving red line earthward. And the sounds, unnatural sounds, anti-life sounds — the sputter and crackle of flares falling into bushes and among the grunts, the once-in-awhile crack of ambushing rifles, the thunk-thunk of Sergeant Herr's mortars, the whine and whump of artillery, and overhead, the droning spotter plane, the extended belch of Puff's guns.

The grunts felt good, reassured, doing this kind of work knowing they were being backed up by Puff and Phantom jets and Navy cruisers and maybe the battleship *New Jersey* lying offshore, and even a battery of the U.S. Army, "those good old worthless fucking doggies." And, if by some fluke something went wrong to reverse one's fortune in the bush, the American grunts could count on a short helicopter ride back to an air-conditioned hospital and the care of real doctors.

For one side tonight there were thousands of people, well trained in specialties of support, willing to leave a television program, a cold beer, a

USO show in the clubs in the rear, to jump into planes or choppers or gun turrets and help the grunts in the bush. For the other side, there was none of that support — no ships reaching fifteen miles inland, ño all-weather jet fighter-bombers, not even the faintest hope of a big shiny Freedom Bird to take them from the war after a certain number of days. If he got ambushed this night, it would probably be better if the NVA soldier died here in the stream named Song Ngan, for survival meant the agony of several days of crawling back into the DMZ with wounds unattended. And if he made it to an aid station alive he could expect to be operated on by a fanatic better trained in the politics of peoples' liberation than medicine. If there were no ambushes there were the endless humps south, the hunger, the malaria.

George Sorenson, Sergeant Herr, the Army, and Puff kept up their turkey shoot through the night. For five hours it was nothing but:

"That last bunch was right on them — I could see the helmets and arms flying... Now go left five-zero and add two-five, six more . . . ."

"Roger that, One. Six rounds for effect — left five-zero, add two-five . . . ."

Thunk—thunk—thunk—thunk—thunk—thunk.

"Beautiful . . . you're right on . . . I can hear them laying out there just moaning and groaning . . . Give me twelve more there, over. . . ."

"Roger that, One . . . ."

"No, wait, Disregard . . . There's some getting away from the blue line . . . add two-five . . . rounds away . . . rounds away . . . rounds away . . . ."

When dawn came Sam went down to the ambush site with second platoon for an assessment and a piece of whatever action remained. For the next three hours he kept the four squads on line and swept through and around the streambed, flushing the remaining wounded from the draws and folds in the cratered landscape, from behind the few small bushes. The pattern of this mop-up went beyond the pathetic, almost to the ridiculous: none of the remaining NVA able to move offered any resistance to the oncoming grunts. They either cowered in terror as their boyish faces absorbed the point blank rifle fire or they turned and ran up the barren slopes a few steps before having their backs and legs shattered by the bullets. Killing was unbelievably easy this morning — the grunts raced one another to drop each new enemy who tried to raise his hands or run. The next day the full account made its way around the lines.

"Yeah, it was just like practicing up for the range — we'd get some from the prone position, then the sitting, from one knee, standing up. Hell, it was easier than the damn range! No way you could miss them. You should have seen Chief do in this one slope that was trying to give up — he just stared him down, flipped his cigar ashes on the guy and blew his head almost clean off!"

Since this grim business was being carried out by human beings who had been brought up in a society which encourages individualism, there was more than one reaction to it. There were some who just did it, who years later would explain it with the old it-was-him-or-me line. There were some who couldn't get enough of it fast enough; those who wanted to kill and then carve initials on lifeless chests, or rearrange facial features. And, there were a few who were repulsed by this killing that was too easy, a few who wanted it stopped. These last few realized what Marines are supposed to do to an enemy in war, but they also realized that the bounds of reason were being crossed this morning. A valuable chance to take prisoners and possibly save other American lives was being ignored. But Bravo was out in the bush by itself, miles away from witnesses, and Sam was all alone with his victims, miles away from criticism. Only once did the outside world come close to finding out about the one-sided battle. Halfway through the mopping up, Sam received a radio call from Herb Marriott of second platoon. Marriott had just seen a grunt shoot an unarmed and wounded NVA soldier who would have made a good prisoner.

"We ought to get as many of these guys as we can, and send them back for questioning, don't you think?"

Sam was in no mood to debate matters he considered peripheral to the opportunity at hand. "Get off the radio with that kind of talk! We can't have the whole damn world listening in. Get back with your outfit."

By ten o'clock Sam was satisfied that he had found all the NVA there were to find. He turned the four squads around and headed back up his hill to call battalion with the body count: nineteen dead and one wounded, the latter a good intelligence prospect. Then the killers were turned into work parties to collect all the enemy gear worth sending back to division. It came to one rocket launcher with six rockets, fifteen half-pound blocks of demolitions, over twenty packs full of rice and personal possessions, six AK-47 rifles with several hundred rounds of ammunition, and a complete 61-millimeter mortar. Next to the bodies, the mortar was the most valuable prize of all, since it could fire the smaller American rounds and thus augment the company's firepower. It was nicknamed "moaning and groaning," after George Sorenson's comment of a few hours before on the condition of his victims. Sam officially ended the ambush by distributing among first and second platoons and the mortar crewmen the enemy packs, belts, canteens and personal effects of the newest victims in an old war. "Here, Chief, you take the gook's money and letters. I want his belt — you can tell by the buckle he was their lieutenant last night."

The score of the night's action would be a challenge for even a communist propagandist to report and explain. While losing at least twenty soldiers and hundreds of pounds of war supplies, the North Vietnamese Army could exact from the marines no more than a few hours of sleep. No one even twisted an ankle on the way back up the hill with his souvenirs.

The rest of the day was spent in fondling souvenirs and "blowing Zs." Around four o'clock a chopper came out. It took away the wounded prisoner and captured weapons after unloading mortar ammunition, water, C-rations, and a new second lieutenant. Later that night there was another I've-got-movement-over-here plea but no human forms came out of the dark. The Song Ngan continued on its way toward the sea as it had for centuries before this American unit staged an ambush on its banks, but for the next three days its brown water took on a reddish cast it had not shown before.

What had occurred in the first ten hours of May 22 at grid coordinates 055669 was something that should not have happened to the proud young warriors of any nation. But it did, and for the marines there was a beautiful vengeance in it all: the thousands of grunts who had stepped on all the box mines and booby traps and pungi stakes in the past five years had died like this too, without the chance to fight back. The grunts gorged themselves on the good taste of it in the next few hours. Then after lost sleep was recovered, as they looked again at the souvenirs claimed from bodies and packs — the pictures of North Vietnamese girl friends and families, the letters — the grunts of Bravo came to reflect more deeply on what they had done. Things hometownish and emotional, things right and natural in an adolescent sort of way came to mind. "Christ, Tony, did you

see the look on that slope's face when he took that last round?" A few realized that at this same time on another hill somewhere, North Vietnamese
soldiers were triumphantly sifting through the pictures and letters of new
American casualties. An unvoiced question here on Hill 130 was "How
can I hide my girl's pictures so no NVA ever puts his dirty commie gook
hands on them if I buy the ranch?"

Fewer still reached the bottom level of these reflections and came to see
the young Vietnamese they had killed as allies in the bigger war of individual existence, as young men with whom they were united throughout their
lives against the big impersonal "thems" of the world who would make
the grunts in a few years think they could never make it big. The grunts
knew there were things that caused people to lead different lives. From
their parents they had heard the nervous excuses, the flashes of resentment when they had first asked why some people lived in bigger houses
than others, why some people wore dress-up clothes to work. A few of the
grunts now saw their dead enemy as comrades in the struggle against the
realities of weakness within themselves too painful to admit, brothers in
the struggle against the faceless and nameless forces of circumstance which
would send them to the union hall instead of the country club, which
would keep them at the gas station, the factory. In killing the grunts of
North Vietnam, the grunts of America had killed a part of themselves.

8

Hill 174

The Company mortar section, now four tubes strong with "moaning and groaning," began the morning of the twenty-third by firing over 200 rounds in the direction of the day's move north. The move turned out to be another of the rare enjoyable humps. All 800 meters of it were under a cloud cover. Since they were getting so close to the DMZ, battalion was telling all four company commanders to stay off the more prominent hilltops. Sam set Bravo in on a finger coming off a hill about 170 meters high. There were comments about what a benny it was not to have to climb all the way up, but there were also comments about being fired at or attacked from higher ground in the night. The routines of digging in and cursing everything in sight and mind were altered somewhat by the universal realization of the Company's new position — 1200 meters from the Z. The sounds of talk and laughter were less audible; those of digging incoming holes a little deeper, more prominent. But the new diligence was relieved in midafternoon when the great green chopper arrived from Quang Tri. There were bennies for everyone — carrots, orange juice, C-rats, lettuce, tomatoes, oranges, water, grape juice, cucumbers, canned hamburgers, three sacks of mail, one man returning from R & R and four slackers from the rear.

One of the most popular grunts in the Company was Corporal Anthony Stankiewicz, just returned that afternoon from his rest and recreation leave in Singapore. Everyone knew Stanks as the kind of marine and friend who would give some of his water, even his prized can of peaches, to any other grunt who said he needed it, who really needed it to go any farther on a hump. But no one ever asked for it. Just knowing it was there, bouncing up and down on the humps, having its paint chipped off by other C-rat cans, sustained a lot of grunts during their time in the bush. Stanks was glad to get back to his friends in the bush and Bravo was glad to see him again. For the next two days the grunts would tell him about the big ambush and he would tell them about Singapore.

Stanks loved to take pictures and he had promised everyone he would take plenty while he was gone. The anticipation of seeing the album of new polaroid shots made it easy for the grunts to forget where they were, what they were close to.

"Hey, Chief, you seen Stanks' pictures yet?"

"Not yet. Red Mountain's got them. Says our squad gets them after we're done digging in."

"I ain't seen them yet either, but that guy what humps a radio in the first platoon says they're really outa sight."

For those who had not yet been on R & R or in a pornographic movie house, the pictures were a little "outa sight." There were two postcard-like scenes of the city and then dozens of snapshots of the marine and his five-day girl friend in their hotel bedroom. In each successive picture ("Fucking A, Man, turn the page!") there was less and less clothing until Stanks and his girl with the name that would be forgotten in a few weeks were down to doing their basic thing of life and love, down to doing what was the reason a grunt dreams of his R & R, counts the days and hours to it. "Oh Christ, how did that feel after seven months in the bush, Man? Look at him going at it in this one — get some, Stanks! Put it to her, Pal!"

When the study of R & R pictures became difficult in the light of a dying sun, Sam called his platoon commanders and sergeants together for a meeting. The session was approached warily, since for only about the second or third time on the operation Sam was smiling and laughing. "Listen to him — I bet he got permission to take us into North Vietnam, probably all the way to fucking Hanoi!" Sam was wearing the small nervous smile worn by an adolescent asking his favorite girl for his first date. He was sitting next to his incoming hole but he still shifted as if on legs weak with nerves. A trace of a blush came through the dark Indian complexion. "Good old Mustang Six sent us a message here and I want to read it here to you now." It was a message of congratulations for Bravo's ambush two nights before: I therefore commend your Company . . . professionalism . . . maximum use of supporting arms . . . dealt insurgent Communist forces a heavy blow." The proud Captain tried to make his reading of the message sound as officious as the typed words but it didn't quite come across. He pulled his mustache, pinched his lower lip and scratched his cheek a little harder but it was no use — that small smile kept growing, kept betraying the pride in the career, the pride in mastering the doctrines " . . . while at the same time sustaining not one American casualty . . . credit to Corps and country."

"So go on back to your areas now and take this message back to the troops — I want every one of them to know the big people in the rear think they done all right back there. Okay, that's it."

There had been more satisfaction in this day than in a long time, more than anyone had a right to expect. Usually whatever satisfaction one found had only one source — some mail, maybe a beer or Coke. Today, however, there were three sources — Stanks' pictures, the Colonel's congratulations and a quiet night.

May twenty-fourth dawned clear and cool. It looked like today's would be the second tolerable move in as many days. "Two nice humps in a row — that's unreal. Now it'll probably rain for two days straight."

"Maybe, but that's in the future. Take all the bennies you can get right now."

The mortar section fired 225 rounds in the direction of the march and Bravo stepped off to the north. In a few seconds the day's temperature did an about-face, from cool to very hot, as three incoming mortar rounds landed within twenty-five meters of the column. After hugging the earth and finding no wounds, the grunts got back to the hump at as fast a pace as loaded packs would allow. Sam and his Company were no longer alone in the green hills; their every move would now be watched by the unseen adversary to the north.

After sending three rounds at Bravo, the North Vietnamese turned their tubes a few hundred meters to the west and gave Charlie Company a few rounds. This time they were right on target and Charlie had to call in choppers to get four emergency medevacs out.

The new position was different from the last two in a way terribly obvious to the grunts. They were not on an inconspicuous slope coming off a larger hill, but right on top of a peak all too prominent, Hill 174. Bravo was dangling right in front of North Vietnamese binoculars and gun tubes. Walking over the top of 174, one wanted to duck as if moving in front of a movie projector so as not to draw any undue attention. Now the grunts crouched 300 meters from the Z.

Besides its prominence, the thing most obvious about Hill 174 was that it had been home for someone else before. A trenchline zigzagged across the eastern half of the hill, partially overgrown and filled in during the past few months. The trench and the discovery of a red-soled shoe made the previous occupants North Vietnamese. The grunts established a perimeter and sat down to study the terrain to their front for unfriendly movement and listen for enemy mortar pops, the muffled pings that give warning of enemy rounds on the way. Two hours later, with nothing sighted and nothing heard, Bravo dug in. During the afternoon of getting the new position ready for night, there occurred the only semi-humorous incident that would ever happen for this American Company on Hill 174.

Earlier that morning, when telling his platoon commanders where the Company would be going, Sam had pointed out "the hill with the white tree on it." The dead barkless tree had been an essential landmark to the grunts approaching 174, but now its height and color made it just as obvious to enemy gunners as it had been to Bravo earlier. It was probably only a matter of time before it would become an aiming stake for the NVA. Demolitions could not be used to bring down the tall white spire — the noise and smoke would give away Bravo's exact position. There was still a chance the Company had not been detected and that chance must be preserved as long as possible. The tree looked rotten but it exacted much sweat and energy before succumbing. First they tried pulling it over with ropes but it would not come down with five, ten, fifteen grunts pulling and sweating. Then they tried hacking it down, using entrenching tools as axes; only the E-tools broke.

For one of the very rare times in their history the Marines decided to fall back from a mission. They said "screw it," and swung Tarzan-style from the short remains of branches. The tree had become another rare benny, allowing the grunts to forget the DMZ, the NVA, and the war for a few precious minutes. It was once again like climbing trees and racing go-carts back home in the summer. There was no longer any choice about the method of removing the tree. Demolition charges would be used to blow it a few minutes before dark, as the mortars registered their night defensive fires outside the perimeter. The old white tree had shown a tenacity the marines came to admire. It had preserved an existence beyond life through twenty-three years of war and was not about to give it all up without protest. "Fucking thing don't want to come down. Well hell, let's leave it there . . . leave it alone."

An hour later after the escape from war granted by the tree, the grunts were jerked back to it all by their sister Charlie Company and the NVA. Around three in the afternoon mortar pops were heard. The scream went round the perimeter — "Incoming, hit it!" — and one hundred thirty-eight young filthy bodies scrambled for seventy foxholes. The grunts uttered short hopes and fought to stretch steel helmets down over shoulders and knees. Twenty-one seconds later the dominant feeling was relief as they heard the karump-rump-rump hit on somebody else's hill. After the initial impacts the grunts raised heads to see where it was hitting. They watched in awe as the rounds were walked up, on top of, and over the hill Charlie Company occupied to the west, a uniform twenty meters between each burst. Karump-rump-rump from the north side of Charlie's perimeter across to the south, six splashes in a row scattering packs and ponchos and water cans and bodies, then a shift a few meters to the west and six more in a row. It ceased only after some twenty rounds had neatly perforated the hill, leaving a geometric pattern of destruction, death and pain. Fifteen minutes later the medevac birds were hovering over the neighboring hill. Feeling awe for the deadly accuracy of one's enemy is no way to begin a night, or a day, in a combat zone.

The sun was down. The grunts held their breath, held it to listen and stare, breathed again. Talk was low and of the essential — of cars that would be driven back home, schools that would be attended, girls who would be taken. The thoughts were from the television generation, from those to whom death had never been a close possibility. "If I get it I wonder what my last words will be?" The fear now felt was the old one about the neighborhood bully waiting around the next corner to wash your face in the snow. All sounds became those of the enemy.

"Hey, Johnny, what was that?"

"Relax, that's a rock ape."

"My dying ass — that's a gook!"

"You throw a frag out there and the Captain'll have your dying ass."

"Yeah, but we gotta do something or he'll just crawl up here and slit our throats!"

"We are gonna do something, shit-for-brains — we're gonna shut the fuck up and crash before the real stuff starts tonight."

Now the DMZ was felt, really felt. Nowhere else in South Vietnam, nowhere else in the war that had no front, did a line on the ground mean what it meant here. No matter where a bush company stopped and set a defensive perimeter, the grunts knew the enemy might be out there, and then again he might not be out there. The enemy might attack each night, and then again he might not. There was considerable room for uncertainty in one's favor, for hope. But sitting on a hill 300 meters from that pink line dividing one kind of Vietnamese from another kind, one could feel how the spaces normally allotted to hope and luck were now greatly constricted. There was simply no doubt about it here: the NVA were out there and they would never let any American unit sit around so close to the land they drew life and strength from without doing something about it. Never.

By some miracle the NVA granted Bravo a quiet night. Coming out of a light, nervous sleep, the grunts again felt the atmosphere loaded with imminence. Consciousness was back; Hill 174 was back. All was quiet here, as if the grunts had ventured onto a tender place on the earth's body and she was holding her breath at their intentions.

Things happened in fairly quick succession on the morning of May twenty-fifth. At seven-thirty a chopper brought out a pallet loaded with mortar ammunition. Half an hour later a second bird brought out thirty cans of water, two R & R returnees, and took from the hill one man due to rotate back to the States and one for R & R. Around eleven, Sam began sending out his first patrols. Two weeks before, a squad leader from second platoon told Sam that before he rotated back to the World, he wanted to take his squad into the DMZ — it would be something nice to tell the guys back home. For about the same reason, Herb Marriott said he would go with the squad. So Corporal Lonnie Bradley took nine grunts, a machine gun team, a medical corpsman and his lieutenant north.

Since the pink boundary line on the maps was not on the ground, Bradley didn't know exactly when he crossed into the Z, but he soon had a good idea by the new look of things. The squad found trails used less than a day before, maybe only a few hours before. They found small campsites where North Vietnamese had eaten and slept and crapped. They found hastily abandoned fires with ashes still warm and smoking. Marriott called the findings back to Sam, "Yeah, well that's okay. Go on a couple hundred more meters and call back." The trail showed more use the farther the Americans intruded. Almost simultaneously Marriott and Bradley concluded they were on the trail of a mortar crew, and it was very possible they could capture it. An enemy mortar would be a nice trophy for the Company — it couldn't be much farther. So in they went, deeper and deeper, still seeing the campsites with rice scattered around recent fires, still finding footprints, rice bowls, discarded clothing. Finally Marriott's sense of responsibility got the best of him and he called Sam again for advice. As near as he could tell, they were about a click into the Z. For nine rifles, one machine gun and one radio that was deep enough. Nothing smaller than a battalion should go any farther. Bradley and Marriott decided to leave the war trophies to others.

Eight hundred meters later, with Hill 174 in sight and its perimeter only about 500 meters away, the North Vietnamese chose to confirm to Bradley's squad that they had indeed been on the trail of an enemy mortar. The first round was some fifty meters short. The grunts were almost in a full run when the second and third rounds hit. They, too, were short, and the enemy purpose was understood. They just wanted to play with the grunts a little, remind them that a real live enemy was out there, and chase the Americans back onto their hill.

At one in the afternoon Sam went out with his second patrol, to the west. They had been out about two hours when Marriott called a third time, reporting his squad was back on 174. Sam and his grunts were finding nothing to compare with the evidence of enemy activity Bradley had seen. In a few more minutes the difference in findings would be of no consequence.

A mortar increment is a small cloth bag, four inches square, containing an explosive charge. Attached to a fin assembly, a cluster of increments propels a mortar projectile to its target. Desirable firing distances are obtained by both adjusting the angle of the mortar tube and detaching from the round one, two or three increments. When ignited outside a gun tube the increments do not explode but burn, very fast and very hot, and thus present a constant fire hazard around gun pits and ammunition points. Once started, an increment fire is nearly impossible to stop.

Private First Class Vincent Pavone, Jr. was an ammunition-bearer and he was getting impatient. His can of hot dogs and beans was taking longer to heat than he was willing to wait, so he decided to add a couple increments to the trioxane ration heating bar under his can of lunch. The irritation Vince felt rose dramatically when he saw the increments melt the can, and dump his boiling lunch in the dirt. He then saw the fire run across the floor of the gun pit from one increment bag to the next until it settled in a pile of empty ammunition boxes and more loose increments. The junk pile flashed into flame and now posed a new and larger danger. The pallet of mortar rounds brought by chopper five hours before, not yet stored underground, rested only a foot away from the fire. If the fire spread to it, Sam would have much explaining to do and many letters of condolence to write. The mortar section leader hollered to the company executive officer, Mike Lancaster, that he had a fire in one of the pits, and several grunts ran up to help put it out.

The rising smoke on Hill 174 was as obvious to the North Vietnamese a few hundred meters away as it was to the grunts fighting it; the former recognized it as a rare opportunity. Now, on the warm afternoon of May 25, 1969, there came to the North Vietnamese within range of Hill 174 a pay-off for the uncounted months of endless marches through roadless jungles, dragging thousands of pounds of food and equipment on aching, bleeding backs and shoulders; the months of eating cold, clammy rice day in and day out with only a little rotten fish and a few drops of *nuoc-mam* sauce to add some taste; of suffering from the dysentery and malaria without proper rest or drugs; of dying on nameless hills, in unrecorded valleys and streambeds; of cowering in terror and hatred as the B-52s and Phantoms roared overhead at will, dropping an array of weapons designed to do nothing else but snuff out their small quiet lives. Now would come a reward no mortar crew in any nation's army had a right to hope for. At two in the afternoon a North Vietnamese Army assistant gunner let one of the heavy red rounds he had carried for weeks slide down the long tube on his Russian-made mortar. With a brain-jarring wham, the round shot into the hot clean air, lifted over the wounded land about 3180 feet, pointed its nose southward and began a long whistling descent.

The mortar pop was easily heard by all the grunts in Lancaster's fire-fighting force, and caused fear and conflicting orders to replace discipline and organization.

"Incoming! Back to your holes."

"No, we gotta get that fire in the pits out first."

"Get down, get down!"

"Get your ass up here on this fire."

"Fuck the fire, it ain't going nowhere — get in the holes, get down . . . ." Twenty-nine grunts raced for their foxholes; thirteen stayed to fight the fire.

The speed of descent of the enemy mortar round and the earth's rotation were such that after twenty-one seconds in the air the round would not land in the dirt of Hill 174; instead, it crashed into the top of the pallet of ammunition next to Vince Pavone's gun pit. An explosive chain was initiated as the round smashed through the top row of ammo boxes, and one-thousandth of a second later the main charge went, setting off the whole pallet, over 2500 pounds of high explosive. Hill 174 shook as in a death rattle and then for Bravo Company the world turned into a dark chaos of noise, dirt, hot metal and blood. The hill lifted, then fell back down in a rain of dirt, helmets, hot shrapnel and human limbs, dragging the chaos through longer and longer minutes. Even before the thunder of that massive explosion reached the ears of astonished North Vietnamese gunners, the dying was over. Whoever was in charge of such things back in the World would now have to send thirteen recruiters to thirteen pairs of parents with the news of Hill 174, thus causing thirteen ministers or priests to conduct thirteen memorial services, and thirteen undertakers to arrange thirteen more funerals.

But the North Vietnamese were not through with this American Company. The hill with the dark brown cloud hanging over it was now a target hard to pass up, difficult to miss. Twelve more rounds crashed into Bravo, adding to the day's wounded-in-action total. There could easily have been more, and without effective retaliation for some time, since Bravo's mortars were wiped out. But for an unknown reason the NVA decided they had done enough for one day.

Sam and his two squads had started running back to the perimeter when they heard the ammunition explode; they reached it just as the NVA mortars quit pounding the hill. Now they ran around to find corpsmen, platoon sergeants and squad leaders and get them functioning again to find and treat the wounded and get things ready for the medevac birds the radioman was calling. It was soon obvious the day's action was over, and survivors began crawling out of holes half-filled by the giant explosion. The grunts looked around trying to recognize the hill whose face had been so drastically altered. They saw chunks of flesh and boots and packs and rifles scattered indiscriminately. Walking down off the crest they began to find the dead and the wounded, dazed and moaning in the grass below. Some had been blown a hundred meters off the hill. All who had stayed to fight the increment fire were dead. Of those thirteen bodies, ten were found.

With death and pain all around, the living fell into a variety of roles and exhibited a variety of reactions to this day. As they looked for and recovered the wounded, some fell back on a religious discipline, some just fell apart and reverted to a dazed and preadolescent disbelief; they felt a superficial joy in refuting the obvious. A few held a stoic dignity, then joined the most serious of games in war, deciding who should have the privilege of giving his poncho to wrap the bodies of friends for their final chopper ride. And there were the ever-present emotional athletes — always ready with a mawkish sentiment at the drop of a helmet.

Four choppers ferried between Hill 174 and the Third Medical Battalion hospital at Quang Tri for the next hour and a half. Those untouched by the blast searched the grass and brush for victims, then carried the limp forms up to where the birds would touch down. Up the hill with a body, turn around and back down for another, up again.

"That's all I remember that day after I came to — carrying guys I knew up that hill in a poncho. Up and down, up and down, all day long. I was in a daze all day, I didn't know what was happening — I started thinking like the whole world was like this and I was doing normal things."

134

Only after the last medevac bird took off was the final casualty count known. It came out to thirteen dead and twenty-eight wounded. The dead included two short-timers. One was Lance Corporal Alan Owens, a Kentuckian due to leave in eight days. In her last letter, his fiancee had reported that the wedding and reception were all set. The other short-timer was Corporal Stankiewicz of recent R & R fame. He was scheduled to leave in five weeks. Most of Stanks' body was found but nothing remained of the treasured album of R & R photographs. By the way he went, Stanks provided Bravo Company with one of the saddest war stories any grunt ever heard, or experienced, in seven years of war in Vietnam. He got the wound the grunts dread the most, the one they have occasional nightmares about. Stanks' abdomen, groin, and legs had been peppered with white-hot shrapnel; he would certainly lose one leg, maybe both. But the larger fact here was that Stanks would never again participate in the ecstasy he knew on his R & R, the celebration that involved every cell and voiced every dream — two sweating bodies climbing to a mind-blowing orgasm. His R & R would always be the last time — at twenty years old, the last time.

Stanks had regained consciousness only a few minutes after the incoming ended. "That's okay, Stanks, no sweat. You're gonna make it just fine — no problem, Pal." The excessive encouragement made no sense to him; they continued to answer his questions with evasion. "Gonna be all right, Stanks — don't worry about it now . . . no sweat, Pal." When he saw where on his body the corpsman was working, Stanks knew what it was.

"What's it look like, Doc? Tell me, goddammit, I gotta know!"

"Lay back there, Stankiewicz — we'll take care of you, you're gonna be okay."

"Tell me, Doc — goddammit, you gotta tell me — I gotta right to know!"

"Take it easy, dammit, you're gonna be all right. You're going back to Third Med and they're gonna fix you right up fine."

Corporal Anthony Stankiewicz died on the chopper, in the air somewhere between Hill 174 and Quang Tri City. The thought of "never again" was too big for Stanks' young mind — he died because he didn't want to live, and the rest of the Company understood. "Fuck it — can you blame him? When the gooks blow away your balls there ain't no reason to live anymore. I wouldn't want to live like that, would you?"

Lieutenant Mike Lancaster also died on the chopper ride back to Third Med, but those who saw him said it was better that way. His body from the waist up had been turned into a lump of carbon.

The luckiest among the medevacs were those whose bodies were missed by the shrapnel but whose brains were temporarily rearranged by the noise and shock of the massive blast. They were brought into the emergency room, stripped, examined and carried to the shower room for a wash-down. While awaiting ward and bed assignments they were placed on stretchers in the corridors. There on the cool cement they babbled and moaned at the ceiling through the night in their nakedness.

Those who yesterday morning had tried to interpret this new place and the atmosphere of Hill 174 had their answer now. This was the place where all things sacred for their familiarity would be disrupted forever in short horrible moments none were prepared for. Now the grunts of Bravo Company 1969 had seen Yorktown and Chickamauga and Belleau Wood and Tarawa and Pork Chop Hill. All of those other battles and Hill 174 came to look alike on this warm afternoon in May. The new generation was blooded.

Today the veterans were reminded and the newbys knew at last — this is where body counts come from. They didn't all come from a last glorious charge to take the hill and plant the flag. The relentless formula was still at work. It was the adding together of six or ten or two dozen Hill 174s each day that had for five years allowed the young voice in Saigon to tell the world: "The U.S. Command in Saigon announced today that scattered actions with enemy forces accounted for three hundred fifty-eight Communist dead. American losses were described as light."

The grunts have a favorite warning among themselves, used mostly in jest, sometimes not. "Payback's a medevac" is another way of saying that any deserved retaliation will be serious enough to put the victim in need of a medical evacuation to a hospital. The promoters of this red-on-green, America-in-Vietnam spectacle had decided that nineteen dead and one known wounded North Vietnamese from the ambush of four nights before would cost the Americans thirteen dead and twenty-eight wounded. Payback really was a medevac.

In seasons past, the coming of June had been a time of joy for the grunts. Only a short while ago — only last year for most — June meant the end of school, the beginning of a new freedom in the sun; no more bitchy teachers, no more dull assignments; just climbing trees or drinking in the back seat of a buddy's car or spending your own money and not telling the old man where you're going. In this June there would be a new order. From the interminable routine of patrols, C-rats, humps and dreams, all overhung with the corrosive uncertainty about when the next firefight would happen and who would get zapped in it, the men and men-children of Bravo moved into a time when they could taste relief. Now it was known who would get mangled and killed. That earlier wondering had drained off a little energy from each man in the last few weeks, in addition to the humps and the heat. Now the mystery was over — after the big blow the grunts had more dead, a measure of relief, and faces which looked twenty years older.

In the next few days the uncertainty that has always been a part of every grunt's thinking came back. This time, however, the wondering was not about who would get hurt and who would go untouched. This time those who had survived were trying to figure out what meaning, what lesson should be taken from the freak disaster on Hill 174. Only one answer was readily apparent — pallets of ammunition must be broken down and placed in bunkers immediately after they are received. Beyond that there was nothing — nothing to be learned from a lucky shot by the enemy and no way to defend against another. Some days our side makes a lucky shot and some days their side makes one — is that all it meant? No matter how many minds thought about it, what happened on Hill 174 didn't seem to mean anything, and that was the most maddening aspect about it. No meaning could be derived from thirteen deaths, twenty-eight injuries and an extensive rearrangement of the landscape. How could anyone be expected to retain his sanity in an environment producing that kind of event?

Only one survivor in Bravo ever voiced his assessment of Hill 174. Two weeks after the lucky shot the second platoon sergeant, Staff Sergeant Melvin Rabbers, was sitting in the Battalion Staff Club at Quang Tri. Rabbers, scheduled to fly out the next day on his R & R, leaned across the pool table and whispered in a loud beery voice to his first sergeant that there was "At least one good thing come outa that pallet blowing up back there — at least that worthless, chickenshit sweater of an XO, that panicky bastard Lancaster is dead, too. Fucking panicky turds like that always get some good troops killed, always happens . . . always happens . . . ."

At Sam's meeting that night there was little more than hope. "Christ, we better not get hit with any more lucky shit shots like that. Another one could knock everything outa the Company for quite awhile. The troops're scared now, talking about the way the gooks did it. All right now, go on back to your people and talk to them . . . calm them down. Don't let them get the idea the gooks can't do nothing wrong, or some stupid idea like that. Remind them about the ambush."

War is as big and horrible an event as man has yet devised to touch a massive number of lives at the same approximate time in an unforgettable way. But no matter how large any particular war has been, there have always been thousands or millions of individuals able to preserve an existence untouched by the chaos and carnage. The number of people not in Vietnam, but directly touched by the deaths and injuries sustained by Bravo on Hill 174, was only about one hundred twenty-five, making generous allowance for the size of immediate families. Thus on May 25, 1969, over 200 million other Americans were wrapped up in experiences other than war or the mourning of its victims.

*   *   *   *   *

While the grunts of Bravo Company struggled with a freakish but deadly happening, millions of other people were doing millions of other things back in Uncle Sam's Empire of Average Men. In Glastonbury, Connecticut, Roxanne Madden was trying, and failing, to kill herself by gulping oven cleaner: she had decided her life was a failure because it was becoming more obvious every day she would never get married. In Malta, Illinois, Ora Rugg was sitting on the floor next to a grocery store magazine rack, absorbed in a *Police Gazette* story about a 1934 axe murder in a Texas border town. In Sweetwater, Oklahoma, Grace Boomer deviated from her diet; it was the forty-seventh time in the last two months she had gone over by one thousand calories or more. And in Tiffin, Ohio, Lester Plant rocked back on his bar stool in Isola's Tavern and hollered at the country and western band ("all the way from Toledo, the Blooo Notes, featuring Wanda and Hubie!") that he wanted them to play his all-time favorite, *I've Got Everything I Need to Drive Me Crazy*. As he crumpled onto the floor and the beer splashed over his face he bellowed, "or if you don't know that one, how about *Kiss An Angel G'Morning*?" And the rest of the world plodded through another work day, gave birth or awaited the final sleep, read their newspaper and cursed their neighbor.

9

Hill of the Angels

Finally, away from Hill 174. This time not one man bitched at the word to saddle up. The grunts humped out under unusual circumstances. Everyone knew where they were going and everyone knew how long it would take to get there: Con Thien and five days. That was a slow pace, an average of only a mile a day if they went in a nearly straight line. It either meant a lot of patrolling on the way or a lot of slack. But right now nobody seemed to care which of the two possibilities they would have to carry out. It was enough just to savor the fact that they were leaving, putting Hill 174 in the past.

Sam took his time and followed a meandering route that tended to the northeast. There was none of the frantic idiocy of humping to nowhere that there had been on the first few days of the operation. There were no heat casualties either. When Hill 174 was two days into the past, some

141

outward signs of life began to return to the Company.

The grunts resumed their bitching at the heat, the hills, and the lack of cold beer and hot broads. Once in awhile a laugh could be heard and Sam had to start passing the word back down the column to "hold the goddam noise down; you're not home yet." The patrols weren't too bad either. They were always short, especially if they were to the north: the DMZ was still only 600 meters away. And since they were moving toward the sea, the hills got lower each day. It was at the end of each patrol and each hump that a new spirit could be seen growing in Bravo One-Three. Each man felt it in himself and watched it in the actions and faces of his buddies. Earlier they were hurt and afraid, individually and collectively, but out of that hurt there now grew something new. It was the bare determination, not to take this hill or that one, but to survive this hell, to outlast that little slant-eyed, rice-powered bastard they chased no matter how many hills had to be humped or how many monsoons or 118° days had to be endured.

Captain Sam's traveling road show walked into the south gate of Con Thien late in the afternoon of June first. June, June — another name for another bunch of days, a little closer to the Freedom Bird. A small convoy of trucks rumbled past the column of troops. Each truck was full of artillery ammo and each pulled a water tank. The grunts had seen all of this before, but what struck them now was the water splashing out the top hatches of each trailer. It was just splashing out onto the Nam dirt, with nobody screaming about wasting the precious liquid! If there was enough water to splash all over the damn road, there might be enough for showers. No, wait — no sense getting hopes up about the bennies without being sure.

Bravo joined the rats that afternoon in the ring of perimeter bunkers. The grunts, the transients, and the rats — the permanent personnel — eyed each other warily, as established residents eye newcomers. Once again the rats lost. They can tell when the marines move out for good, when flak jackets and packs are picked up for the last time, not for another patrol. They must think, hopefully, at last, this bunker and the garbage dumps will be ours with no more traps laid, no more pot shots taken — ours at last. But a few minutes later here come the next occupants.

Tired bodies, exhausted minds slept through the next dawn. With the earth starting to heat up again, Corporal Denny Sayre of Avondale,

Arizona, stumbled out of his stinking, sandbag-lined bunker number 18, squinted into the big orange ball moving up over the barbed wire and radio antennas, stretched his arms over his head and screamed as loud as he could, "Good morning, Vietnam!" Thus began the war's next day.

The name Con Thien translates as "Hill of the Angels." Considering the variety of small pleasures and the relatively low number of losses the grunts would experience in their four weeks at this forward outpost, it did seem as if the place were being watched over by divine beings.

In the next few days the grunts settled into quiet routines with plenty of room for the bennies — steaks on a charcoal grill every night, mail with an occasional bottle of booze from home, plenty of Z time and showers and ice cream and cold Coke and movies, and only a couple of rockets every few days from the NVA. One of the best bennies turned out to be the details sent back to Third Med at Quang Tri for dental appointments. While some grunts had their teeth fixed on such details, others found the dentist too busy and, "the dental tech said we'd have to come back again tomorrow or some time. Gunny, I know that sounds like bullshit but it's the truth, Gunny, honest!" The rest of the day was spent in finding a boom-boom girl — "Hey, Chief, let's go in the vill and get the old pipes cleaned out, eh?" — and a bottle of whisky and maybe some grass for the rest of the squad.

The bennies at Con Thien were so good and the occasional rockets from the north of the Ben Hai River so poorly aimed that the change coming over Bravo at Con Thien was barely perceptible. Much more than the morale and combat efficiency of the Company was changing. The unit once called "Bloody Bravo" was taking on a new character and a new identity. Three and a half weeks at a base near division headquarters was enough time to receive thirty-one new bodies. A few weeks before, the blooded veterans, the old-timers of the war and the Company, had been those who were "down south on Taylor Common back around Christmas." Now those who had survived the explosion of Hill 174 were the real veterans. A bare thirty days ago was suddenly "way back before we ever had any of this shit here like steaks and ice cream and movies and fucking showers." Then would come the final attention-getter for the newbys: "And don't get the idea it's gonna be like this all the time — you ain't even barely seen the bush yet!"

After a few days, after the newness of the Stateside bennies wore off, there wasn't too much excitement for the grunts in their weeks at Con Thien. One source of entertainment was "firing up the rats." Traps were improvised in the garbage dump at night, the rats collected the next morning and held through the day. At sundown they were doused with diesel fuel or gasoline, set afire and turned loose. "Looks real cool at night, them old rats screeching and running around in circles. Don't know where the fuck they're at. Then they just stop dead, roll over on their backs and just crackle and simmer — ha!" After the last few weeks, the grunts had grown numb to suffering and death.

Other breaks in the routine were provided by the occasional NVA rockets 500 meters off target between eight and eight-thirty in the morning, the NVA skeleton first platoon found draped over the outer perimeter wire one morning, and that shoving match one night in the chow line that never really turned into a fight before the lifers stepped in. It wasn't over who would get what steaks — there were enough for each man to have three in each meal if he wanted that much. The real issue turned out to be an argument about whether Two-Four had saved Three-Three's ass at the battle of Jones Creek the previous spring or whether Three-Three had saved Two-Four's ass. It was important to get your war stories straight before they were taken home and told to girl friends, children and eventually, grandchildren.

Those incidents weren't much considering they were all that was produced in thirty days by over one hundred and sixty grunts virtually locked behind barbed wire — with no broads, either. But that was just fine with everybody. There had been more than enough excitement for Bravo in the month before they got to Con Thien.

Rounding out the routine bennies were the patrols. They averaged out to just one every other day. Most days they reminded one more of a high school class trip to some historic shrine than a search for the enemy. Patrol routes were keyed to debris left over from the hot summers of '67 and '68 — days when Leatherneck Square was filled with battles between, not snipers and ambush squads, but battalions supported by tanks and artillery on both sides. Battles for Con Thien were among the few, in the five years of the American involvement, during which the North Vietnamese Army felt it necessary to stand and fight, not only in the night, but during the day when the Phantom jets with their 250 and 500-pound bombs and their napalm could be called in from Phu Bai and the Seventh

Fleet carriers in the Gulf of Tonkin. Sam would simply say, "Take your squad out the south gate over to the west to that there tree-line, then check things out around that burned-out chopper. Then go over by that shot-down jet . . . ."

Only one patrol during Bravo's entire stay at Con Thien was remembered as a real bummer. The morning after they arrived at the fire base, Sam took three of the four platoons on a sweep completely around the perimeter. The hump turned out to be fourteen clicks long and took nine hours, which made it the worst since those of the first three days in May. The Company had found several tank trails and the debris from earlier battles, but no NVA and none of their rice and ammo caches.

The first sign of enemy activity was found by Staff Sergeant Jerry Goodman of third platoon and his radioman, PFC Herman L. Hopper. Three days before, Goodman had the dubious honor of being named acting platoon commander while his lieutenant was on R & R. Acting leader is not a sought-after position among the grunts, since they, along with radiomen and corpsmen, are much preferred as targets over riflemen by the enemy. What Goodman and Hopper found was an old mine. They found it in a manner not recommended in the field manuals: they stepped on it — without ever seeing the little green plastic trigger sticking up among the blades of grass. About half a dozen bodies were lifted from the earth and scrambled around. The only two who died were Goodman and Hopper. The NVA weren't even around but they still got the right people.

The mine accomplished just about what the Russians who made it and the North Vietnamese who planted it had in mind. The only things left inviolate on those two human bodies and their clothing was the propriety of boots on feet, though the feet were ripped from their legs. The mine mixed trousers with calf muscles and tendons with genitals with intestines with bladders with shit with livers and spleens and kidneys and stomachs, and jammed the oozy mass up into lungs and throats. Then it burned hands and arms and chests and faces to the texture and appearance of dried prunes. Just like it was supposed to do.

There was no longer any doubt about what warfare in the modern, industrial era had come to mean. The grunts — newbys, short-timers, and lifers alike — could see now that what happens to human beings in mechanized warfare has absolutely no poetic or theatrical possibilities. Fuck you, John Wayne!

Lance Corporal Roland Epps and the rest of his mortar crew were there when Bravo Company walked into Con Thien back on June first. Troops from different units usually don't mix very fast, since all are taught that theirs is the best battalion or company, and "if you hang around with them other horseshit outfits, anything's liable to rub off on you." But here was something of a special situation. Only a few days before, it was announced that Epps' unit, Second Battalion, Ninth Marines, would be taken from Vietnam as part of the President's withdrawal policy. So, very quickly, Epps of Two-Nine met the grunts of One-Three. Almost every day the grunts ambled over to Epps' mortar pit, ate Cs with him and helped him get things ready to go, as if by thus associating with and helping these short-timers, some of their shortness would rub off and help them get home sooner. They shot the shit with these mortarmen from another unit, shot it all day long. And at night they got together behind the perimeter wire and sang their favorite song, the one about getting out of this place if it's the last thing we ever do.

At first there were questions like "Bet you're glad to be leaving this fucking place, huh?" That one turned into "What you gonna do soon as you get home?" and "Smile if you're gonna bang your girl — ha!" which led to, as do all conversations between marines, "How did you ever get in this green mother anyway?" Roland Epps of Austell, Georgia, had quite a story to tell, for his family and the Marines had been together a long time. It was a story the grunts long remembered.

Elton Epps, Senior, was the first in his family to enlist in the Corps, back in 1888. The high point in his twenty-year career was his service in the Spanish-American War. He later tried to go back on active duty against the Hun in World War I; he was lauded for his patriotism and graciously turned down. Next was Elton, Junior, who enlisted in 1920. A promising career, and one he loved, was cut short when his first wife made him leave the service after only eight years. But his younger brother Elbert stayed in for twenty-five years, retiring in 1947. It was Uncle Elbert's endless stream of war stories of the Pacific campaigns that first planted, and then kept alive and burning, young Roland's ambition to join the Marines the first chance he got.

The third generation of Epps marines was represented by Elton III, who joined in June 1950. Four months later he was in the newest American war, the Korean "police action," and two weeks before Christmas of that same year, he was killed in the freezing withdrawal from the Chosin Reservoir. On May 31, 1950, Elton, Junior's fourth wife gave birth to his fifth child and second son. He was named Roland and on his eighteenth birthday he became the fourth in his family's direct line to join the Marines. He had wanted to enlist the day after his seventeenth birthday but his mother made him promise years before that he, unlike any of the other Epps marines, would graduate from high school.

Four months later he was in Vietnam and assigned to the 81 mm mortar section of Two-Nine. On June 25, 1969, he was at Con Thien along the DMZ with his mortar crew. The day before they had been told they would be re-deployed to Okinawa with the entire Ninth Marine Regiment. There had been rumors, but here it was at last ". . . the fucking President was gonna let us skate right on outa the Nam, forever! I couldn't believe it, Man. I didn't know whether to shit or go blind, so I started packing!"

The jeep and trailer had come out in the morning from Quang Tri for the mortar, ammunition, and the seven crewmen. They had planned to be back to Quang Tri for lunch in the mess hall with its cold milk, so Epps and the rest of the crew threw their C-rations into the grass behind the gun pit as a way of underlining and celebrating the fact that they would never again have to eat the meals that come in green cans, the crap that tasted lousy and gave one as much diarrhea as nourishment. But packing the trailer took longer than expected, so they decided to have that one last meal out in the bush.

Everyone at Con Thien, including Roland Epps, knew there were mine fields both around the outer perimeter and inside the wire in the fenced-in grassy areas. But those mines had been there over three years and probably didn't work anymore, and besides, they were going home — the President and all the heavies said so. So Roland Epps walked out into the grassy area behind his bunker with nothing more on his mind than finding the can of beans and franks he had thrown away two hours before.

The "Bouncing Betty" anti-personnel mine is one of the more brutal products of American military technology. When triggered, it doesn't explode in the ground and take feet off legs. It springs up four feet before it goes off, and separates heads and arms from bodies and perforates lungs, stomachs, and intestines. Lance Corporal Epps' Bouncing Betty picked him up and, while he flew through the air, ripped off his clothes, legs, hands, and all of his head but the lower jaw, then dumped him on his back — stumps of thighs and arms raised in supplication to a garish sun. The first man on the scene told a corpsman that he thought he saw a pink mist hanging over the corpse for a few seconds. In the last possible hour of the last possible day in the least sensible of all way to do it, Roland Epps had won his plastic body bag with the big long zipper. About one hundred twenty of their son's one hundred seventy-two pounds were sent home to Mr. and Mrs. Epps.

*   *   *   *   *

While at Con Thien there were people like Roland Epps, Jr., elsewhere and doing other things were people like Frank Parks. While the former's last and violent noon was ending, the latter was spending his as he had every other noon for the last three years. He was standing at the corner of LaSalle and Adams streets in Chicago, waiting for "Don't Walk" to change to "Walk."

When he wasn't waiting for lights to change, Frank was working in a bank. And when he wasn't working in a bank, Frank was engaged in what he considered the important things in life — picking up secretaries at his favorite bar, furnishing his apartment, driving his new Corvette, and keeping himself in the latest clothing styles.

Like Roland Epps, Jr., Frank Parks thought about Vietnam, but much less frequently and in completely different terms. To Frank, the war was an annoyance, an unpleasantry. And if not handled correctly, the war could also be a threat to his social life. He learned very quickly that those who injected the sordid subject of war into parties soon found themselves beating the bars alone. After about ten seconds of analysis, Frank decided to leave the war to others and to concentrate on more important things, the activities centering on that mad race of the unmarried, the swingles circuit.

Frank Parks was pleased that after analyzing his life to date, he could conclude he was generally in step with the procession of his generation: his feet were in motion and his brains were at rest. He fit the mold of the partly-educated hedonist, the image he consciously admired. Frank was "on his way," as they've said the last few generations, but on his way to what, he didn't know.

148

*   *   *   *   *

In the early afternoon of June 25, Sam had a meeting with all of his platoon commanders and sergeants. After the death of Roland Epps and C-rations and beer and dental appointments and test-firing of weapons and the rumors about the next operation had been discussed, Sam added one more piece of information. "Oh, and tell your people Operation Virginia Ridge officially ended at midnight last night. I don't know what the next op's gonna be called or where it'll be, but we'll probably be walking outa here in a few days, so tell them to be ready."

part two
The World

To those who fight for it, life has a flavor the protected never know.

anonymous, written on a C-ration case at Khe Sanh, 1968

During the twenty-three days at Con Thien, six grunts reached the end of their tour in war. For these six there were new joys in this next summer of the war. There was the first sergeant's gruff "You're leaving tomorrow — be at the CP ready to go at zero-nine." There was the beer — and maybe pot — party the night before; there were good-byes and address changes; the last chopper ride, the last overhead view of the emerald and pock-marked Vietnamese countryside; a real shower in the rear; another drunk; a C-130 flight to a larger terminal. And then the most fantastic sight of all — a big shiny 707, one's own Freedom Bird, walking down the runway, nose bulging through heat waves, swinging around, doors opening. "All officers and civilians of equivalent rank followed by E-6 and above form a line over here, E-5 and below this side . . . Good afternoon, gentlemen, welcome to Continental Air Lines government contract flight . . . I'm Shirley from . . . will demonstrate the life jackets to be found over . . . ." As the bird raced down the runway, one hundred eighty-five pairs of hands and feet tensed against plastic and carpet, straining to feel every pebble and indentation in the strip, straining to feel the exact second of lift-off, the exact moment they could put Vietnam and whatever it meant to them in the past.

At the instant of separation between Freedom Bird and Vietnam, a cheer rose throughout the cabin. The new ex-grunts felt the same mix of relief and exhilaration they had felt dozens of times before in the past year when they received a letter, began their R & R, and ended each of the dozens of patrols and humps they had made. But this was the biggest hump of all, so the exhilaration was raised to a higher power than ever before. Within a few minutes voices died away as the new veterans leaned back to savor the sweet fact of leaving, really leaving.

Shortly after they reached home, the six new veterans and many parents and girl friends of those still at Con Thien, began writing letters about some special news coverage the grunts were getting. It was like no attention they had ever before been paid. The editors of Life *magazine thought it important to give an impression of the Vietnam War that would go beyond the usual shrill protest or caustic editorial. They wanted to report, not only the number of dead for the week, but exactly who did the dying on those days. So in its June 27, 1969, issue the magazine staff printed individual photographs of 217 of the 242 American servicemen killed during the week of May 28-June 3, 1969. The pictures and names filled thirteen pages in addition to the cover. Six of the 217 pictures were of Bravo Company marines killed on Hill 174 the afternoon of May 25.* Life *called the article "A Record and a Tribute."*

The grunts called it something else. They were hurt by the article, openly resentful about the way Life *treated their dead of that week. They were probably more bitter than other units represented in the pictures, for they had not yet found the chance to avenge their loss. After things were evened up the grunts would be glad to show America and the world pictures not only of their own dead but those of the enemy who would be riddled and blown apart, posed with and perhaps mutilated. But until that day, death would remain to these grunts a private thing, something to be faced and shared with only the closest of friends. Death was not to be displayed or advertised in any way, for any motive.*

"What the fuck's going on back there? They think we actually groove on this kind of shit? They don't do nothing for a guy till after he buys the ranch. Then all the pictures get put in the papers and magazines. Really nice, eh? They ought to send every one of them mother-fuckers over here — put them right in the middle of a firefight — see how they like it! Fucking civilians back in the World don't know what it's like over here — don't want to know — don't care. Just so that they get their new car every year and their cold beer and a hot piece of ass every night!"

10

Our World and
The World

Just as the Vietnam War was different from any previously fought by Americans, so was the experience of returning from that war different from any other. Soon after they had settled back into families and neighborhoods, the newest veterans could see that all the Hill 174s and Khe Sanhs and Hamburger Hills could not be left completely behind.

Virtually all the veterans expected that their settling back into familiar places and routines would be one of the most pleasurable experiences they would ever know. But most found the process to be a succession of painful adjustments to a way of life which contrasted sharply with the one they had just left behind in Vietnam.

Consider only the larger contrasts between the war and the home society: where the veteran once could afford to be concerned with only the next few moments or days, he now had to formulate plans that would affect him for years or decades. Where he once had to make only one or a very few decisions to survive, he now had to make many decisions about many different subjects — and those sometimes in the same day. Where there was once the ultimate penalty for mistakes — death, there was now only a casually administered system of rewards and punishments. And where the veteran once had only a few very close friends he could always count on, he now moved in a much larger society of short-term acquaintances, almost none of whom were willing to make any deep commitments. Thus, coming home amounted to living through an experiential blowup.

The last of these contrasts was for most the first felt. The impact of the loss of close friends is well illustrated by only a brief statistical analysis. During the entire period of direct American military involvement, about 2.5 million troops served in Vietnam. Once back in America, those 2.5 million were dispersed within a population of over 200 million. Thus, the veterans had only about a one percent chance of meeting each other. Back in the World the veterans were surrounded by persons unable to understand their thoughts, their actions, or even their words.

The veterans' first few steps back into the world of things relatively peaceful and conventional might have been taken at a transient center on Okinawa, where they found billboards offering "Thanks from a grateful nation for a job well done." It might have begun at airports in El Toro or Fairfield, California, where they found Red Cross ladies serving cookies and coffee, and VFW volunteers passing out handshakes, congratulations and key chain charms stamped "Welcome Home, Your Country Is Grateful." Or it might have begun at reception centers in Oakland or Seattle where they were required to listen to welcoming bands and speeches. Wherever such introductions to their postwar America occurred, the ex-grunts noticed a common feature about them: they were contrived events, not spontaneous. They happened because base commanders ordered them to happen. That was something of a tip-off, a signal that it might be a good thing to be a little wary of America, to put off for a few days embracing the things they had missed and expected to be the same when they got back.

From their first few impressions on returning home, some veterans concluded America was as beautiful as ever. Some found it indifferent; others found it hostile and ruthless toward itself and its newest veterans. The latter two of these three groups deserve considerable attention for, having stepped outside and then re-entered American society, they are among the few able to provide some commentary on how the war affected the idealized view of themselves Americans have long held.

Contributing to the impression that America was full of hostility, was the fact that in the latter years of the American involvement a large number of veterans, perhaps over half of the returnees, came back hating something or someone: the Vietnamese for being so unfathomable, so generally "fucked up"; American politicians for lying to them about why they had to go to Vietnam; hippies for "stabbing us in the back"; and the Joe Blows and their housewives who went about life as usual while the grunts had been counting off their hours and days in the paddies and hills. Along with the hatred were mixed generous amounts of fear and suspicion. Was it true that hippies were going around shooting every Vietnam veteran they could find? Was it true all the girls thought the veterans were baby-killers and would have nothing to do with them? When the veteran learned those rumors were not true, his suspicion still remained; and it was, he felt, justified.

Back in the States, he felt alone, naked, exposed to the dumb peering and probing of those afraid to get involved with things outside their own life-cocoons. He wanted to be left alone to heal his wound, to "get his thing together," so he could somehow face tomorrows that looked too bright, too hard. But they — the newest adversaries, those who hadn't gone — wouldn't let him. They kept boring in, sticking him in the private parts of his experience.

No matter how sincere the concern of family and friends might be for the veteran's smooth adjustment to a peaceful environment, it was usually received as an assault, an aggression on his peace of mind. The best thing most could do in the face of such assaults was to anticipate and try to head off the dreaded questions. Many of the veterans adopted a new method of judging others. The test was simply, were you there? If the answer was no, the barriers went up.

"What was it like?"

"It was a bitch most of the time — sometimes okay. Hey, I heard you got a new car while I was gone."

But while almost every veteran devised some defenses against probing hometowners, he also ran into one or two friends who wouldn't be put off, who really wanted to listen and understand what it was like. Genuinely interested listeners were a welcome change to most veterans, but after hearing about the war in the bush, most were left with a squinched up face and in a mood which momentarily precluded eye contact or sound.

"You really want to know what the Nam was like? Well, okay, I'll try to tell you. It was like a big-ass greasy machine with plenty of parts but it don't do nothing. You been to a big discotheque, haven't you? Well, throw in a lotta that psychedelic crap and people doing stuff they don't know why they're doing it and they wouldn't do it anywhere else, and then throw in a big bummer trip on LSD with no up, down, right, wrong, yes, no, left or right, new or old, no noise, no silence, and then add a seventy-five year old VFW jerkoff standing in a graveyard full of twenty-year-olds giving a lecture on the proper display of the flag, and that's about it — a lotta motion, noise, color and smoke but no progress, no meaning."

The superficial commercial and trivial aspects of America were the parts of their beloved culture that hit the young veterans early, and hit them hard: . . . *Dear Ann, your reply to Cheated On who wanted to phone her friend 2000 miles away and tell her that hubby just confessed they had slept together thirteen years ago stank — Will Congress wake up now? — God loves you and has a wonderful plan for your life, call 334-0467 (a recording) — Medical costs top GNP rise — I was troubled thirty-five years with red patches, scaly skin of dreaded psoriasis — gum chewing now legal — Ruth Cobb and Cliff Madden were named today as December bowlers of the month — Why singles are swinging to the suburbs — Austria tries two ex-SS officers for war crimes — Cigarette smoking might not interfere with the development of an unborn child as is widely suspected.*

When Vietnam did make the news it was reported as something far away, of little consequence; it didn't sound like the same event that had almost taken the veteran's life during the past year: *Pentagon is silent on second massacre — Long-locked GI goes on trial in Viet — United States and the Viet Cong clashed today on the third anniversary of the dead-locked Vietnam peace conference . . . Each accused the other side of sabotaging the meetings — Draft dodging Eskimo caught.*

The veterans could easily see the great variety of games and deceptions America plays upon herself daily, all the while thinking she is enhancing her glory, moving closer to the dream realized. Back Stateside the synthetic had resoundingly triumphed over the real. America was on a trip,

158

an endless fantasy journey, careening onward under a garish sun to brighter, odorless, unstained tomorrows.

A view of any nation or culture which dwells on things marginal is of course neither complete nor objective. But such a view says much about the psychological condition of returning Vietnam veterans. What they had done in the year before their return had not prepared them to be objective or generous to a people and country who, most veterans believed, had either ignored or helped make more difficult their trials in the war.

After all that ennui had been waded through and the new veteran had turned off the radio and television, and wadded up the paper and thrown it at the world, there were other things to be contended with, other things a little too big for the mechanisms of toleration and assimilation. An ex-marine from Chicago who left an arm in Quang Tri Province said it for all the veterans.

"Things are more screwed up in the World now than they ever was. Christ, I get back and people are more bananas now than ever. My girl's pissed at me now cuz I don't want to get married for awhile and then I gotta write this paper about the war I don't want to write and — ah shit — it's back to normal. Nothing is like it was supposed to be when I planned it out back there. Seems like they're all coming home now, you know? All the same crazy fuckers we had over there are back now and screwing up the World.

"Yeah, this instructor I got wants me to write themes and essays about my experiences in the war. He asked me if I ever saw a gook up close or shot one I could see, and I says hell, yeah, I did. So he says write about it. He says I should write about what I was thinking when I was doing some of the crazy shit we did over there. I can't think of any reason — not one — why I shot the guy — nothing — except maybe to stay alive but no, shit I don't know . . . .

"But I think the worst change was the broads. You know how we used to think about them and talk about them back there? Well, I knew they'd be different, but, Man, I didn't think they'd be that different. About half of them didn't even recognize me at first and then they say stuff like 'Oh, you were on the basketball team weren't you; no, the football team wasn't it?' Then it's crap like 'Gee, I bet you're glad to be out now,' and 'When do you think it'll be over anyway,' and when you're about halfway through answering them they kind of half turn and start to drift off and then if you try and talk with them again or ask them out they get real snooty, like, anybody's had any connection with the Nam, they don't want nothing to do with them.

"It's like when a guy decided he wanted to go to the Nam, he dropped outa life or something. But then they feel free to flash their ass in your face, and when you make the natural, normal reaction and try to get some of it, they act surprised, like you're trying to do something civilized people don't do. Snooty fucking bitches. I'm even thinking of going back to Hong Kong where I had my R & R and finding the girl I had — I know right where to find her. She's got these bitches around here beat all to hell, all to hell."

From life and death to snooty bitches and a pile of rubber, steel, grease and vinyl from Detroit called "Something To Believe In" was too great a distance for the veterans to cover in sixteen hours, or even sixteen days. It could be done physically but not mentally. Few could quickly assimilate that stark dichotomy, few could quickly move away from it and formulate those things their parents call career goals.

The veteran took the mountain of ennui he found in America as evidence that the hometowners didn't really care what he had gone through in the previous year, didn't care about the buddies he lost or those still there when he came home. Such extreme apathy was inexcusable to him. And if he asked people why they weren't stirring from their routine he heard an answer that compounded his bewilderment: "Vietnam's been going on ten, twenty years — how can I afford to worry about it all the time? I got too many other things to worry about, and if I did think about it all the time, what could I do about it? I can't change the world by myself. Marching and writing letters to senators don't do no good at all — it don't change nothing."

The veteran's bewilderment at the civilian reaction to the war revealed a large flaw in his observation of those who did not go, and in what he did with that observation. The hometowners were no more interested in Vietnam when the veteran they knew left home than they were when he came back. The civilians were thus consistent and logical in their own minds. It was the veteran's sense of commitment, his definitions of logical and rational that had changed by his participation in the war and so, on his return from it, he criticized civilian attitudes he had not even noticed before he went. If that inconsistency struck him at all, it was usually passed off with the comment that his lack of prewar criticism for civilian America was "before the Nam showed me what things was all about." But whether or not there was a flaw in the veteran's thinking, his analysis of civilian America was no less real to him: apathy about the war was still inexcusable.

After seeing his buddies blown apart, his country refuse to unite behind his war, and hearing many at home say his buddies died for nothing, the veteran badly needed psychological anchors on which he could build some kind of adjustment to his recent past, and on which he could base a value system that would serve him in the future. In their postwar America most veterans found none of the anchors they so desperately needed.

Most of the veterans then fell into a period of condemnation of the "fucked-up civilians getting their ass every night and rodding their hot cars around." Many found themselves going out of their way to insult home-bound civilians. For many, the period of condemnation turned into one of wandering. There was a strong revulsion against staying in one place too long, seeing and hearing the same people too long, watching the same deodorant commercials and hearing the same sports announcers mouthing about the "life and death" importance of this game and how many hundred thousand dollars so-and-so is holding out for.

Staying in one place too long built up a rage that could not be contained for the sake of courtesy or any other arbitrary value; a rage that drove the vet to move on, to gulp down the next experience . . . and the next . . . and the next. The rage pushed them into an accelerating succession of friends, parties, girls to conquer, places to see . . . more and more . . . faster and faster . . . according to no plan and with no visible end. Some had to leave the country to get away from the land of contradictions, warped values and hypocrisies, away from the America they no longer recognized, that barely showed any awareness of and no interest in what they had done for their own vision of America the Beautiful and Pure. For many there seemed nothing left in America for "our kind." It looked absolutely insane and hopeless to try and make any sense out of this place and its "fucked-up civilians" who didn't care what their country was doing to another people ten thousand miles away.

Why couldn't they just say, "I don't give a damn about what you did, about your friends who got zapped," instead of faking their concern and asking their questions while their real concerns were elsewhere. The civilians just couldn't do it, they had to go on asking their shallow questions — Is it really hot over there? Are the people really as small as they look in the papers? Is it true the Vietnamese don't value life like we do? What's the monsoon like anyway? When are we going to win? Do the people eat anything besides rice?

The veteran's desire to condemn and escape America revealed another flaw in his thinking. He assumed that all the fault, all the inability to understand what he went through, lay with the civilians, with anyone who did not go. The veteran, however, must share some of the blame for the resultant misunderstanding. He assumed that Vietnam, or war, was the only really enlightening experience in life, because Vietnam was that kind of experience for him. Unless one had been there, he was automatically an incomplete individual in several ways. The personal frustration the veteran felt when attempting to explain the experience of war to others confirmed that belief. The veteran forgot, or discounted the fact, that before he went to Vietnam he was equally inexperienced at interpreting and describing events. As big as that flaw in his thinking was, it remained functional and led to certain decisions by the veteran about how he would exist with his postwar America.

These flaws in the new veteran's thinking illustrate the difference of the returning grunt's orientation toward the war compared to the attitude of those who did not go to Vietnam. Both veteran and hometowner were looking for something when the former came home, but neither was able to satisfy the other's need. What most veterans did not see on their return was the deep frustration Americans felt over the course of the war. The richest and strongest nation in the world was not bringing a "small" war against a small and underdeveloped country to a decisive conclusion, and those who had not seen the war wanted to know why.

The veteran, however, could give no satisfying explanation. He was unqualified by experience to explain how decisions had been made in the White House or in State and Defense Department policy planning sessions over a period of nearly two decades. He was also unqualified by temperament to ease the frustration he found — he returned looking for consolation, for understanding. Instead of offering what the veteran needed, the stay-at-homes asked about the failure of national policy: "When is it going to end? How did we ever get involved in that thing anyway?" When the veteran talked about the only thing he was qualified to talk about — what his war in the rice paddies or the hills had been like — the frustration of the hometowners was only compounded. What followed then was a mutual withholding of what each side needed. Since the hometowners found in the veteran no relief for their frustration, they withheld their consolation and understanding. And since the veteran found no empathy in the hometowners, he withheld any attempt to understand their views.

Vietnam gave most grunts a clearer view of themselves and America. Life in the bush had lain them bare for themselves and everyone else to inspect, and moving outside of America had given them a chance to see what most of those who would never leave would never see. On his return the new veteran could see several stark contradictions about America he had missed before. He also noticed new contrasts between himself and other Americans. For one, there was a big difference between his and others' ideas of what is important in life. In the shopping center, Mrs. Schmitz might feel free to make it known to the clerk, an ex-grunt, that she must have a light blue sweater just like that gray one for her husband's birthday or, "my Roscoe will simply be beside himself." Answering the obligations of his job, the veteran will push through his mouth the words, "Yes, Mrs. Schmitz, I understand completely — here, let me help you find it." But in his mind he formulates and holds his true sentiments on the matter: "The world ain't gonna blow up if you don't find the fucking thing, Mrs. Schmitz. Why don't you tell old Roscoe to go screw himself for his birthday?"

Much larger contrasts and hypocrisies become visible. Americans pay most of their professional athletes more than their cancer researchers, marine biologists or ecologists. In some parts of the country Americans seem unable to decide if teachers or garbage collectors are more valuable members of society. And no matter how much the politicians babbled on about equal protection under the law, those with money always got more equal protection. More painful to the new veteran was the discovery that there were millions of Americans protesting bitterly the loss of 55,000 American lives in Vietnam over a period of ten years while those same protestors, and millions more, quietly accepted the same death toll in one year — every year — on American highways. It didn't make much sense to the veteran for people to reject 55,000 deaths but accept 550,000 when the elimination of both was well within the realm of possibility. And Americans are great ones to holler about the need to eradicate organized crime, but when it comes to acting against it they come with all kinds of excuses and dodges such as "leave well enough alone, don't trouble trouble," and "I can't take on the whole mafia by myself . . . besides, I'm too busy raising a family." To the untrained and longing eye, absent for one long year, it appeared that America the land of a better life had become America the land of "if you don't see it, it doesn't exist."

Considering the rapid change during the 1960s in black Americans' views of themselves and their rightful position in American society, it cannot be surprising that the black grunt on his return found even bigger hypocrisies. The American dream and its documentary accompaniment about all men being created equal and entitled to equal protection under the law seemed more a joke than ever before suspected. It takes little effort on the part of any member of any race to imagine the deep rage and bitterness a black grunt on patrol in a nameless jungle or sitting in a fox-hole must have felt on hearing that thirty-two of his brothers and sisters had been gunned down in the streets of Detroit in 1967, or that in 1968 his most effective leader in the fight against a second class existence in white, "who-needs-niggers" America — Martin Luther King, Jr., — had been assassinated. At some point in their tours, most blacks came to feel that in Vietnam they were being used to fight "whitey's war." Their resolve, understandably, was to return to the States, where the real struggle awaited settlement, and help settle it. The veterans, black and white, could see they would have to adopt attitudes somewhat schizophrenic in order to tolerate things intolerable but inescapable, in order to get along in America and the world for four or five more decades.

Except for those who didn't notice the world beyond their own families, the veterans had to make some kind of accommodation with the indifference and hypocrisy they found in their postwar America. Many just went along with it and returned to the niche they left before they went to war. These veterans succeeded in suppressing their revulsion for people who feel powerless and accept massive contradictions. Others could neither go back to their old niche nor find a new one. In their wanderings away from the business-as-usual world of those who did not go and could not understand, they withdrew to memories of the deep friendship they found in the environment of war; the friendship that recognized no differences of background, race, education or belief. They withdrew to the time and place in which Whites, Blacks and other ethnic group members could call each other "chuck dudes," "splibs," "bean bandits," or "wops" without a trace of racism intended or detected. These veterans were more than a little surprised to find that the war was taking on the aura of the good old days, for while it was being experienced it seemed to have absolutely no potential for nostalgia. But in one respect it *was* the good old days. It was a time when humans cared and helped each other with no questions asked, for no reason other than the grunts were all human beings facing the same adversity in the same time and place.

After a few weeks and months back in the World most of the new veterans found that their best friend was time — big fat, indefinable, irresistible, all-around-them time. It kept moving on, over times of peace and war, joy, indifference and sorrow, rounding off the jagged edges of terror and blood, keeping the future a realm of possibility and victory over things petty and wrong. Time didn't erase Vietnam from memories, but it granted more room to the things each veteran wanted to remember about this war, and it pushed into smaller and smaller corners those things painful to recall. Time made easier an accommodation with whatever America presented her newest veterans.

For a few, even the passage of time was not enough to make America tolerable. They rejected their home society and its definitions of acceptable behavior. Recounts one veteran, "I was back from the Nam only two days and my sister started screaming at me for the same petty crap she did before I went. 'Pick up your clothes, be back by twelve, don't drink so much, don't hang around with that Perez kid.' So I threw an iron at her and split her forehead open. I was sorry after but I thought she deserved it. No — hell I don't know." Most of the actions stemming from a rejection of things familiar in America were confined to the circle of family and friends, but some such acts could not be so contained.

There are some grounds for the conclusion that whatever difficulties the veterans had in adjusting to civilian life were the result of their own imaginations. Many civilians made exactly that criticism after observing what they believed were no more than the rantings and whinings of a bunch of spoiled kids who had run into the hard world for the first time. As has been shown, the grunts were capable of some surprisingly faulty reasoning on occasion, thinking that produced surprisingly ineffectual, even pathetic, actions. But the "rantings and whinings" judgement suffers from being superficial; there were sources of veteran discontent and disillusion other than the imaginary, sources far more concrete.

Virtually all the grunts returned from the war anxious to resume or begin jobs and careers, but economic conditions were not notably accommodating to that desire. The rates of unemployment among all American workers in the years 1969, 1970 and 1971 were 3.5 percent, 4.9 percent, and 5.9 percent respectively. As the withdrawal of American troops from Southeast Asia began and continued, unemployment rates among Vietnam veterans increased sharply and remained far ahead of the rates for nonveterans. The 1969 unemployment rate for veterans aged 20-29 was 4.5 percent; the rate rose to 6.9 percent in 1970 and 8.8 percent in 1971. It was not until the last quarter of 1972 that the Vietnam veteran unemployment rate fell back down to the rate for nonveterans.

Compounding young veterans' bitterness on the issue of jobs after Vietnam service was the attitude of expectation brought home by most. The ex-grunts came home, not expecting ticker-tape parades, but half expecting the country with an international reputation for generosity to offer them a job, an activity that would help them put the Nam in the distant past. When they remembered what they went through in the war, the veterans didn't think they were asking too much. The employment situation they found on their return seemed to stand as confirmation that America really had turned indifferent and hostile in their absence.

11

Preparation

The story of the Vietnam grunts cannot end with the close of another search and destroy operation or with the first few experiences back in the World. The environment in which they grew up before they went to Vietnam must be examined if the grunts are to be understood for what they were in a foreign culture and in the war. The people in that environment did not comprise anything very close to a cross-section of the American population, for America's wars are fought only by the sons of a certain segment of American society. America's wars are fought by the sons of bricklayers, truck drivers, policemen, steelworkers, farmers and telephone linemen. With few exceptions, the sons of working class Americans did the soldiering and the dying in Vietnam.

It has long been noted that particular social classes exhibit particular values. Since the grunts by and large were raised by one socioeconomic group, they were exposed to a set of values unusual for its uniformity. Several features of that value system are easily identified. Working Americans live with much economic uncertainty, most probably because they were much more deeply impressed and hurt by the economic depression of the 1930s than other groups. They generally feel that hard work, not welfare, will keep such uncertainty at an acceptable distance. Success in the battle against that uncertainty is indicated by the continued acquisition of material things. Working Americans firmly believe their country and what they call "the American way of life" are the greatest in the world, especially in the areas of economic and military power. They believe just as strongly that other ways of life — especially communism — deserve their contempt. Working Americans generally view social changes as threats to their own tenuous position. They are suspicious of superficial differences in people, particularly those of race, for racial and life-style differences imply changes and threats.

The Vietnam grunts and the rest of those Americans born between 1940 and 1954 were affected by a series of experiences and developments originating both within and without their home environments. Those experiences did not complete the maturation of those who would go to Vietnam, but they did contribute to an attitudinal framework from which reactions to subsequent experiences, like the Vietnam War, would be formed.

The first experience was being raised by their parents. Those who had been touched rather heavily by depression and war in the 1930s and '40s resolved to spare their children as much of such suffering and want as possible. Most parents succeeded a little too well. In their zeal to relieve their offspring of the painful parts of life, the grunts' parents created a generation shielded from much of what has steeled every previous generation — the realization that a certain amount of adversity not necessarily deserved will be encountered in the course of one's life. Two events of the 1960s illustrate this particular lack in the preparation of young Americans. The more politically active members of the postwar generation were actually surprised when they got their heads cracked at the Democratic National Convention of 1968 for demanding that the political heavies of the country simply give up their hard-stolen grip on one of the major political machines of the modern world and retreat to retirement. The kids ignored, or never found in their casual studies, one of the bigger lessons of history — right rarely wins without might. And, many young Americans could go to the Vietnam War with the incredibly infantile notion that they had a *right* to return from the industrialized carnage alive or in the same condition in which they went. For most of their offspring, the parents of the postwar generation had perverted the American Dream to mean 24-hour protection from reality and other unpleasantries.

The timing of the younger generation's lifetime played a part in their preparation for life: they grew up during a period of high tension between the world's super powers. The Cold War made it easy for the grunts' parents to pass on to their children a hatred of communism. Through the late 1940s and 1950s communism appeared to most distant observers to be a united international conspiracy bent on the quick conquest of western civilization. For convenient proof, Moscow poured forth a steady stream of threats about catching and surpassing, even burying, the West. But the Cold War also made easy the questioning of the older generation's virulent anti-communism. For one thing, the younger generation was not trying to defend an idea they had held for over thirty years — it was simply less painful to question. Second, no one could fail to notice that no matter how many threats and deadlines came out of communist capitals, no Russian bombers or ICBMs ever came over American territory or that of a western ally and no invasion fleet ever left a Russian or Chinese port.

The postwar generation was the first to grow up with television, a medium of communication whose profound effects are still not fully understood. In the fifteen years before American ground troops were sent to Southeast Asia, television gave illustration and emphasis to several values and habits of mind that were not helpful to people who would have to adjust to a rapidly changing and increasingly complex world. Television glorified violence and at the same time kept it at a safe distance. The viewer was encouraged to accept the idea that swift and violent action usually yielded positive results. He could also see that he didn't really have to get involved in the problems of others if he didn't want to, he could let somebody else do it. Thus some of the incentive to develop the requisite amount of discipline to face and solve one's own problems was missing from the environment in which most young viewers were growing. The evasion of problems seemed a viable alternative.

Television helped many Americans, young and old, to adopt an escapist mentality. With the aid of television one could leave far behind him the numbing repetition of his own existence. Things unpleasant could be made to seem far away, for other people; things fantastic could feel close and credible. The "boob tube" encouraged both superficial and black and white thinking. Viewers quickly learned they didn't have to exert any effort at analyzing people and events — the tube did it all for them. Nor was much effort needed to distinguish between good and evil. The "good" guy always wore a white hat and rode a white or golden horse; the "bad" guys, dark brown and black. And of course no problem, no evil could withstand the determined attack of the former. Television did much to give the postwar generation a "great-man" interpretation of the world and its events, and by so doing made them vulnerable to the disillusion they found in Vietnam; for one of the notable characteristics of that war was its lack of heroes. All the above negative features of television in its formative years combined to help deprive the post-World War II generation of the kind of experience they needed to deal with either the Vietnam War or the consequences of protesting it — they had been insulated from too much reality.

Three personalities greatly affected the postwar generation in the 1950s and early '60s — James Dean, Martin Luther King, Jr. and John F. Kennedy. All three were, in varying degrees, challengers of convention and all three were assisted in their rise to prominence by the special character of their particular time. The period 1945-1965 was a time in which relations between men were shot-through with insecurity, the result largely of machines taking a larger place than ever before in human communities. During the same period, relations between nations were overhung with the Damoclean sword of nuclear destruction. It was a time of quiet, but building, tension. Since there are limits to the human capacity for tolerating dissatisfaction and frustration, it was inevitable that rebellions small and large against the extended anxiety would be occasionally manifested.

In the young actor of the mid-1950s, James Dean, a new American made his appearance, the personified antithesis of traditional American values. The new hero was the antihero; it was perfectly appropriate that the movie crowning Dean with instant celebrity was entitled *Rebel Without a Cause*. Dean's doctrine was quickly lapped up by young America: throw out the "tried and true," tell off the old man and old lady, drink in every pleasure in life you can find, don't give a damn about anything, and get your kicks now because you might be dead in a little while. Dozens of other celebrities in the Dean mold soon followed, and millions imitated the image of the black leather-jacketed greaser rebel.

White rebels were bad enough for many witnesses but along with James Dean conventional America had to watch a black man assert himself in protest against the lowly place maintained for his race. In December 1955, Martin Luther King led a bus boycott in Montgomery, Alabama, which culminated a year later with the elimination of segregation on Montgomery's public conveyances. Millions of minority Americans were encouraged to a new view of life. One didn't have to wait in quiet resignation for the sympathy and fawning benevolence of those in power to end injustices: they could be ended by direct action.

John F. Kennedy offered living affirmation to the belief of young generations everywhere in every age, the belief that a better world is possible. With his rise, power had finally passed from white-haired, seemingly unimaginative men born in the 19th century, men associated with depression, discrimination and war. In word and act the young President gave strong suggestion that he and those who followed him could answer a universal desire: the aching need to do something meaningful in one's time on the planet and leave some mark as proof for eyes unborn to see that earlier lives had been full of purpose and worth remembering and building upon.

But the accession of Kennedy revealed a weakness in youth of the 50s and 60s. Raised as they were on television, young Americans, and many of their elders as well, had come to be as impressed by imagery as by performance. Young Americans embraced their heroes more dearly than would those who understand how terribly fragile heroes and hopes really are. They thereby opened themselves to deep hurt, disillusion, and cynicism if by some intervention of tragedy, their dreams should not come as true as they did on television or in the movies.

That of course is exactly what happened — all three heroes were taken in early and violent death. The passing of Dean, Kennedy and King left in many young Americans, the feeling that they had been cheated of the brighter future that was rightfully theirs. Other violent deaths of heroes — Malcolm X and Robert Kennedy — underlined the reaction. Many assumed, with little real justification, that the world was reverting to gray older men

171

of shorter vision and smaller purpose, and that injustices would live on.

The adoption of Dean, Kennedy and King as heroes pointed out a fundamental difference of perspective, of philosophy, between youth and their parents. The latter had several decades of experience in living with extra-moral and extra-legal practices such as lying politicians and racial injustice. They had learned to accept such as part of life, they had learned to exist around it. But the postwar generation did not come to the same easy acceptance of the deceptive in life. They resolved to end it. To them, more things moral and just seemed possible. It was the same difference of outlook that characterized almost every other generation, only in the 1960s it was carried still farther.

There were other larger developments witnessed by the postwar generation, experiences so broad of later effect yet so imperceptible in their earlier stages that they almost escaped notice or label. During the 1950s and '60s there was a great expansion of educational opportunity. In 1950 there were six million persons enrolled in American colleges and universities, and vocational schools. By 1960 the total post-high school enrollment had risen to seven million, and by 1970 to 15.7 million. The education explosion indicated that more people every year were determined to translate into reality the legacy of the postwar generation's heroes — improvement really is possible, one is not programmed to repeat in dumb imitation his parents' lives and frustrations.

Permeating the environment in which all heroes emerged and all developments ran their course, and determining much of the individual and public reaction to each, was the collection of values which came under the label existentialism. While they were first stated in the early nineteenth century, existentialist doctrines did not come into prominence until after World War I. The generation born after 1940 has been more deeply affected by existentialism than any other — the philosophy both created the environment conducive to the emergence of individuals like Dean, King and the Kennedys and was in turn given new expression by them. Existentialist doctrines reflect the disordered and tragic character of the past one hundred years, a time of world war and world revolution. The philosophy constitutes a revolt against recent absolutisms — Nazism, communism and corporate statism — which have overrun individual freedom.

According to existentialism there are no universally binding moral laws,

172

no absolute moral values — man creates moral values. Man is considered a finite but contingent being, existing in a world devoid of purpose. Man is also free and responsible, but he is responsible only to himself. Existentialism encourages the individual to believe he can exercise rational control over his own existence, and it offers legitimacy to the questioning of authority figures and groups — parental, religious, social, industrial and governmental — considered unjustifiably arbitrary and absolute. By the 1960s strong currents of escapism and hedonism had been injected into the existentialist spirit and were reinforced by developments such as the birth control pill. The slogans of the youth revolution merely gave word and voice to ideas and activities that had been in practice for several years: *God is dead, Off the pigs, Revolution for the hell of it,* and *If it feels good, do it.*

The experiences of the grunts' early lives held the potential to revolutionize relations with their parents. The values they were taught by their parents were retained, altered or rejected under the influence of different events and personalities than those experienced by their parents. At the risk of misrepresenting the views of some individuals, a risk inherent in all generalizations, certain attitudinal differences and likenesses between the grunts and their parents can be described. Most of the grunts retained their parents' anti-intellectualism and their narrow range of tolerance for differences in others. Both generations are almost equally responsive to peer pressure. Also retained were the views that most changes of routine or thought were too painful to be beneficial and that success was properly defined in materialistic terms. The grunts significantly altered their parents' anti-communism, racism, patriotism and work ethic. Rejected almost completely were the older generation's social morality, particularly their ideas of proper sexual conduct, and the view that the United States alone among nations speaks with the voice of high morality and pure truth.

The events and experiences of the grunts' impressionable years determined how they would react to and perform in the Vietnam War. Since a cataclysmic event like war is so thoroughly unpredictable and uncontrollable, no one is ever really prepared for its occurrence. War always makes extraordinary demands on those it touches. The Vietnam War, however, placed demands unprecedented as well as unusual on those Americans directly involved in it. At certain times the grunts were stalking and fighting an enemy nearly impossible to identify, and that was the task for which they were trained. At other times they were supposed to be under-standing and making friends with a people thoroughly foreign, an assign-ment for which they were not trained. And it was not always clear when either one of those activities was more appropriate than the other. Combat alone would have presented the grunts with the toughest experience of their lives; on top of that was a baffling and maddening culture clash. It is doubtful whether any military force ever faced a more difficult, perhaps impossible, task.

Considering the events and experiences of their lives, most of the grunts were poorly prepared for what was asked of them in Vietnam. There had not been enough hardening experiences which could have tempered them for the most demanding event of their young lives. A surprising number (to this observer) seemed shocked to find that after they filled sandbags for five hours they had dirt under their fingernails; or, when they walked through streams and paddies, leeches sometimes attached themselves to their legs, or when a malarial mosquito bit them they got malaria, or when they were shot at they felt about nine times the fear they ever felt before, or that when human beings get shot they bleed and scream and turn blue and sometimes die.

As a result of the grunts' poor experiential preparation, combined with the absence of a clearly-understood objective in the war, the conduct of the two and one-half million who went was marred by actions — drug abuse, atrocities against Vietnamese civilians, and fraggings among American servicemen — which precluded even a partial accomplishment of their official purpose in going to Vietnam. Even if such incidents occurred only a few times, they would warrant detailed analysis but in Vietnam they occurred on an unprecedented scale.

12

Atrocities — Why?

Every generation has grown up with heroes to worship and big events to live under. Considering the particular mix of people, values, and events which influenced them during their formative years, the grunts, as the corresponding group in every generation, developed both positive and negative capabilities. In the environment of war those capabilities were projected to extraordinary dimensions of both beauty and depravity. The grunts could commit acts of love and acts of hate.

Vietnam presented young Americans with an unprecedented amount and variety of adversity. Besides the blood and death, there were the endless humps under a merciless sun and daily contact with perhaps the most baffling culture to which America has ever sent its troops. There was not enough water, food, booze, women, pay, or sleep; and there was no Honda 350 to jump on and leave it all behind. Every grunt reached a certain point in his tour when the ubiquitous adversity made him aware of two things, the effects of which were almost as sobering as his first experience with hostile fire. He realized, first, that he was fast approaching the limit of his toleration; the anti-adversity armor he had acquired in boot camp was wearing thin. At the same time, he also realized he had no really satisfactory alternatives to the mounting irritations of his existence. He felt he was losing the control of his destiny to people and forces who did not value highly his own well-being. Suppressing his anger and frustration and somehow plodding on was no longer considered a viable alternative. That had been tried before and was seen as no more than an alternative to itself, another deception; it thus became just another facet of adversity. "The Nam and all its bullshit" always came back after each renewal of discipline, each resolve to finish the tour with no bad incidents to stain the record, the memory. That realization was unprecedented for most of the grunts, for television had given their generation the idea that there was an alternative to every adversity, every boredom: change channels or walk away. Such an attitude had no validity in Vietnam. For some of the fed-up, booze was enough to make tolerable the remaining hours and days; for others, it was pot; for others, heroin provided the needed sanctuary. But still others found no relief in those alternatives — they moved on to atrocities against Vietnamese civilians or fraggings of their own unit leaders.

When dealing with a subject as serious as atrocities, it is important not to add to the emotion with which the issue is charged. Such incidents must be put in a proper perspective. It is simply not known how many atrocities occurred in the war, but personal observation and interviews lead me to believe that between one-third and one-half of all Americans who served in Vietnam committed one or more of the atrocities cited below. It should be kept in mind that most of those who served in the war quietly did their jobs without calling any undue attention to themselves, either of praise or censure.

Of the more than two million men who served in Vietnam many gave unselfishly of their money and time to ease some measure of the pain and burden of a standard of living which to an American looks only slightly more advanced than the Bronze Age. Both specialists and non-specialists offered their services to a wide variety of projects in all areas of South

Vietnam. Thousands of doctors, dentists, nurses, and medical technicians spent hundreds of thousands of hours administering modern medicine and teaching basic standards of hygiene, in both large cities and tiny villages, under the Medical Civic Action Program (MEDCAP) of the U.S. Command. Hundreds of clinics, hospitals, and schools were built and thousands of Vietnamese trained to staff them. On their own initiative, thousands of American servicemen spent much of their off-duty time working in orphanages and schools. Thousands with agricultural experience in civilian life volunteered their services to improve and increase grain and livestock production. Thousands with construction or engineering experience planned and helped construct wells, roads, irrigation and plumbing systems, bridges and all types of buildings. And nearly every unit assigned to the war conducted fund drives for the repair of homes, schools, and hospitals following their destruction by one or both sides in the conflict.

When the bullets flew, the grunts were the greatest people in the world to have around. But, between firefights, probably half of the grunts, in their dealings with the people of an ancient and very different culture, were at least counterproductive and often just plain disastrous.

When Americans now think of atrocities, the My Lai massacre comes to mind. But murder was not the only type of atrocity, and My Lai was certainly not the first, only the most widely publicized. There were literally tens of thousands of incidents of malicious intent and atrocious result. Most did not involve murder and only a handful were ever followed by any attempt at redress.

In addition to murder, rape and robbery were common types of atrocities carried out by American troops. Americans on patrols and sweeps often had ample opportunity to pacify a sex drive and engage in souvenir-hunting in private homes. And in every unit were a few individuals, dubbed the "zippo squad," who liked to burn villages to the ground whether or not the combat situation dictated such. In heavily-populated areas there were many who enjoyed riding around in jeeps and forcing Vietnamese on motorcycles or in three-wheeled buses off the road. Others got their kicks by driving close to pedestrians and kicking them into roadside ditches. Still others got a laugh out of teaching hungry young orphans living on the streets how to swear in English, without explaining what the new words meant. Older concepts of entertainment and relieving boredom received new definitions in the context of the war in Asia.

The grisly details of atrocities have been amply documented elsewhere. Here the concern is with the particular values and prejudices which Americans carried to Vietnam and which produced atrocities. There are probably as many different reasons for the occurrence of atrocities as there are individuals who committed such incidents, but four major groups of characteristics and interpretations of the grunts, the Vietnamese, and the war answer most questions of causation.

There were several physical and cultural characteristics about the Vietnamese which set the foundation for an environment in which atrocities could occur. The first thing any westerner notices about the Vietnamese is their small physical size. Half the adult population appears to be under five feet tall and weigh less than 120 pounds. Also obvious to the armed American was the fact that the Vietnamese were unarmed. Those two observations together invited the impression that the Vietnamese were unable to effectively answer injustices done them. Once that impression was reached the grunts fell to the temptation of taking on the attitudes and swagger of the Great Western Conqueror. Abuse has always come easier from those who consider themselves conquerors than from those who consider themselves invited guests.

The language difference between Vietnamese civilians and American troops did much to increase the probability of atrocities. Effective communication between the two groups was prevented for all but the few willing to learn a foreign language in a short time. The two groups thus remained for the most part unintelligible to each other; neither was able to ask the other for explanations of superficial traits that may have provoked wonder, irritation or outright anger. Instead, misunderstanding compounded misunderstanding until the general reaction of each to the other was at least a constant suspicion and at worst a deep anger and hatred. When an American on patrol walked into a village and saw two Vietnamese talking, he assumed they were discussing the best time to shoot him in the back or trigger the booby trap that lay just ahead, not the best time to plant the next crop or the chances of rain during the next week.

The American was confirmed in his belief that Orientals have always been a sly and cunning race, "just like the Japs showed at Pearl Harbor."

When Americans expressed their frustration or anger against the Vietnamese, the language difference worked to the benefit of the former. No matter how loudly the Vietnamese might protest, the grunts couldn't understand; according to the perverted logic of which the latter were sometimes capable, the complaint then wasn't a complaint. Thus, whatever feelings of guilt that might follow an atrocity were either considerably lessened or completely precluded.

On casual inspection, the Vietnamese don't seem to have any definitions for terms like right and wrong, moral and immoral. That erroneous view is reinforced by a number of practices which in America would be punished promptly by social pressure or the courts, but which in Vietnam do not even draw a passing glance. Three practices or attitudes in particular earned the revulsion of Americans in Vietnam: people of all ages defecating in public areas, a monstrous black market operation, and an attitude toward love and sex that is, to those raised in a society which generally values Christian ethics, unbelievably casual.

There were several characteristics about the grunts which helped to bring atrocities to reality. Going to Vietnam represented the most radical departure from the routine of their lives, the greatest possible break with familiarity. Just seeing an underdeveloped Asian country was that much of a change; on top of it was combat. Vietnam hit the grunts hard, for it made them exercise their limited capacity for toleration of things strange more than anything they had encountered before. For many, Vietnam simply presented too many things that could not be assimilated. In such a situation most grunts fell back on a trait of their parents — a quick condemnation of identified differences.

The Americans with the least inclination to be patient or tolerant, and those with virtually no education about a very foreign culture, were exactly the people placed in the position which demanded maximum amounts of those traits and preparations — a daily contact with the Vietnamese people.

The grunts' habit of defining success in materialistic terms, also learned from their parents, contributed to atrocities. Over three-quarters of all Vietnamese live in flimsy-looking huts with no air conditioners, television or stereos inside and no swimming pools or fast cars outside. With so few material things attached to their lives, things the grunts believed added importance and meaning to life, it didn't look like the Vietnamese would be losing much if they were robbed, belted around a little or killed.

Many troops harbored and were capable of expressing varying degrees of racism against non-whites, and nationalistic chauvinism against foreigners. This capability was brought close to manifestation by one of the few historical facts of the war known by a large number of troops: the South Vietnamese government requested American assistance against the Viet Cong and North Vietnamese in 1965. That request was taken by most troops, and many Americans, as proof of Vietnamese inferiority, as an admission of weakness. A related fact, the result of simple observation, underlined that judgement — the Vietnamese did not even seem capable of establishing the prerequisites of national development and greatness: social order and political unity.

The susceptibility of most grunts to peer pressure did much to allow atrocities to continue. On one level there was the unwritten but very strong law that buddies in war do not turn each other in to authority figures — they don't "rat" on each other for anything, least of all for the sake of a few "worthless gooks." On a second level was the fear that one would be considered less than a man if he didn't participate in atrocities with his buddies. Murder, rape, or any form of harassment of unarmed civilians somehow constituted an expression of masculinity to some grunts.

Overlaying all their other traits was the focus of the grunts' minds during their year in the war — they were glued on the day they were scheduled to go home. After 365 days it would be all over — if they didn't get killed or wounded before then. If they kept their date with the Freedom Bird they could forget everything they ever saw or did in the Nam. The grunts became willing to do anything to stay alive until their last day in the war. Nothing within their view or contemplation — taking any unnecessary chances or the lives of Vietnamese — was important enough to delay in any way their return home. At that point the grunts allowed the "Mere Gook Rule" to enter their value system: a crime wasn't a crime if it was committed against a Vietnamese, a Mere Gook. When individuals holding such attitudes were placed in an environment where pre-modern attitudes and practices dominated, the atrocities which could result did result.

Once in Vietnam, with the particular values they brought to the experience, the grunts found several specific tendencies about the Vietnamese which they felt deserved their hatred. They made the predictable mistake of all subjective observers — they judged the Vietnamese against American standards of conduct. Complaints varied with individuals, but among the most frequently cited were: the Vietnamese appeared to have none of the team spirit, long-range planning or can-do determination so admired by Americans; it was every man for himself among them, the only disgrace was to be found out; they expected too much from westerners and were not inclined to take responsibility themselves; they showed no reluctance to break their word unless there was a strong advantage in keeping it.

In addition, there was still another characteristic about the Vietnamese which completely repulsed the grunts. Asian peoples are much less inhibited than westerners about displaying their affection for friends of the same sex. Among Asians, holding hands or walking arm in arm in public does not arouse suspicions of homosexuality. The grunts, however, were shocked at such behavior. They needed to believe their allies and those whose freedom they were supposedly defending were better than "a bunch of queers."

Many troops witnessed incidents which added painful verification to the alleged Vietnamese propensity to lie. Everyone had heard about the patrol that came to a village and was greeted by smiling elders and children. On the way out the other end of the village the patrol ran into a Viet Cong ambush. "Why didn't the villagers tell us about the ambush? I lost two buddies there. Fucking gooks never tell you the truth . . . worthless fucking gooks."

With the loss of friends dominating their thinking, the grunts were in no mood to try to understand the two conditions — one cultural, one military — accounting for such behavior. The Vietnamese do not feel they lie to westerners, since they and most Asians respond to feelings of shame more than guilt. One of the many sources of shame is giving bad news to recent acquaintances and persons not in one's own family. Since one of the criteria of successful (harmonious) relations with others is the avoidance of situations giving shame to either party, the Vietnamese make every effort to give others good news. If that effort involves doctoring or ignoring the western definition of the truth, and if all other alternatives (only slightly lesser deceptions to the westerner) are closed, then the western definition of a lie is given.

A condition imposed on villagers by the war goes farther to explain alleged civilian deception. The Vietnamese populace found itself in an impossible position in the conflict — caught between the war's adversaries, unable to give complete loyalty to either side. With no front line in the war, opposing units might sweep through the same village only hours apart. For the sake of survival, civilians could not afford to give either side any more than minimal assistance or toleration — to help one side too much meant punishment at the hands of the other. Life in most villages was a succession of extortions — for information, food and young recruits by the VC, and for information and suspected VC by the Americans. The villagers thus considered Americans and Viet Cong equally deceiving and exploitive — neither was willing to stay in the villages and offer a lasting protection from the other. But in one respect the VC were less painful to have around — they had no artillery or air force with which to bombard villages by mistake.

Those who came into frequent contact with the Vietnamese had to work around an expression they found on almost every Asian face and one they found very maddening — the perpetual smile that soon became known as the "shit-eating grin." The more frustrating Vietnam became, the less sincere the smile appeared; after a few days or weeks of seeing it, the smile came to look like a sneer especially designed to anger Americans. "I tried for six months to get this guy I was supposed to be advising to level with me on something, anything, but he never did. No matter what question I asked — which way did the VC go, are there any booby traps down that trail, is the village chief on our side or theirs, is your sister a whore? — all I ever got was that shit-eating grin. And one time I even told him one of my squads lost three men in an ambush, and the guy just stood there grinning. I wanted to smash his filthy little slope head and spray his brains all over his fucked-up country. These fucking gooks are sick, Man, sick."

The action by the Vietnamese that angered the grunts even more than the perpetual grin and the deception was the performance, or more accurately the lack of same, of their ally's army in the field. The grunts believed, with strong justification through most of the war, that they were doing more than their share of fighting and dying in a war that was not theirs. To the American grunts, those for whom the war was being fought were doing more running away from it than fighting. There were too many accounts verified by disinterested observers to call that impression the result of emotionalism or imagination. And raising the grunts' resentment to an even higher intensity was his belief, again verified, that the

182

crooked politicians and political generals were spending more time partying in Saigon nightclubs and manipulating the black market to their advantage than they were training the ARVN and instilling it with the determination that might have shortened the war.

Every war has presented certain environmental factors that allow some actions to occur which do not contribute to the accomplishment of any official mission. The Vietnam War was no exception. In war, troops are placed in an environment which suggests they can do almost anything they want and there will be no punishment. Whatever method they choose to express anything from a temporal frustration to a deeply-held racism will, they believe, be absorbed without reaction by the local populace, the country, and the war. The physically and militarily weak appearance of the Vietnamese reinforced such a conclusion. Not only in war but also in peace the strong and partially-educated have never shown much respect for the weak. The discovery that one could get away with abusing Vietnamese civilians removed most of what prevented that abuse. The only other restraint on abusive behavior — a moral standard that reserves no room for it — was either suppressed or not felt by many of the grunts.

In spite of the legends and movies, war never has been one bloody scene after another. There has always been plenty of room for boredom as well. Their past experience with the American standard of living caused the grunts to develop more boredom than they had ever had to deal with before. Back in the World there were girls, fast cars and bikes, and all the music, pot, and booze a guy could want to relieve boredom. And perhaps most important of all, there was freedom of movement. If one wanted a change of scenery he could always jump in his car and head for Florida or California or any place he wanted. But in Vietnam most of those avenues of expression or escape were closed. For some, committing an atrocity offered welcome relief from the boredom.

War and peace give prominence to different people in any society; the former condition seems to bring out all the less reputable types from whatever their peacetime hiding places. For many grunts, the type of Vietnamese they met in the context of the war made a positive impression of the first foreign people they ever encountered nearly impossible. The only civilians many Americans met were pimps, whores, draft-dodgers, black marketeers, informers for the VC or starving street urchins trying to steal the watches off their arms. For many, the logical conclusion was that since Vietnam was full of such types, the "gooks" really were worthless, deserving of hatred and abuse.

At some time in his tour practically every grunt developed a soporific fatalism about the war and his tiny place in it. The first symptoms usually became manifest by about the third month of the tour and helped bring atrocities to reality. "Hell, we figure we might be dead the next minute or day anyhow so what the fuck difference does it make what we do? What difference does it make if we shoot at farmers in their paddies or screw village girls or jerk an elder's beard or beat up a cowboy trying to steal the watches right off our arms? Who would give a shit? And even if they caught us what could they do that was any worse than shaving our heads and sending us to Nam? Ha, we're already here!"

Several special characteristics of the war helped increase the grunts' frustration and thus increased the probability of atrocities. Many believed they were sent to Vietnam to do nothing but kill communists. They were therefore not at all receptive to official directives about treating civilians as equals or "winning the hearts and minds" of the people. "What the hell kind of deal is this anyway? I came over here to fight, not to pass out candy and bandaids to ignorant slopes who don't even talk my language!" In addition, Viet Cong policies of avoiding prolonged battles with American units often made impossible the avenging of a buddy's death. Kept alive long after the VC melted into the jungle, the desire for revenge frequently caused grunts to turn on the first Vietnamese they could find. In many instances, the victims turned out to be children and the elderly. The rationale for such action usually ran something like, "Most of them are communist anyway — the kids and old ones set up booby traps and hide rice for the VC all the time — and they tell them where we are, too. They always know when we're coming and then they get their ambushes ready."

Many of the grunts never could accept the fact that they were not greeted in Vietnam as their fathers and uncles had been received in Europe and Korea — as liberators. The grunt was not, he believed, being appreciated by the very people he was sent to help. Thus, concluding that he was sweating, humping the hills, going without his girl, and bleeding for nothing, the grunt then could commit atrocities more easily.

Finally, no American fighting man ever faced a more confusing enemy than the Vietnam grunts faced in the Viet Cong. Unlike members of the

North Vietnamese Army, the VC wore no uniform. VC looked like civilians, and civilians looked like VC. Many grunts then considered all Vietnamese active Viet Cong, "just to make sure." The difference between suspected and confirmed VC was consistently obscured, often with fatal results for the suspected.

The best one can do to explain atrocities is to come back to one of the general conditions accompanying all wars — the absence of any sociolegal system other than might is right. The lack of a mechanism of redress for the weak gives a psychological justification for abuse by the strong — if a soldier thinks he can get away with abusing others in some way, there is a high probability that he will try.

13

"Take Care of Your Men"

Some of the grunts showed themselves capable of still another negative act — the fragging of commissioned and noncommissioned officers. The deliberate throwing or planting of fragmentation hand grenades by American troops against their own unit leaders was a side of the Vietnam War just as hideous as the atrocities against civilians. It could be said that the misunderstanding, resentment and outright hatred which was manifested in fragging incidents originated in the different socioeconomic background of officers and their men, but such a judgement would ignore the many officers who were once enlisted men as well as the fact that many victims of fraggings were middle and high-ranking enlisted men. The more immediate and telling differences between small unit leaders and troops had their origin in the different training given each.

Junior officers and noncommissioned officers in training are constantly

187

urged to "take care of your men," to "think of the troops first." But troops and leaders settled on different definitions of that concept. To the latter it meant keeping each man functional in a combat sense. To the troops, however, taking care of them meant sparing no effort to soften the adversities with which combat presented them. The platoon sergeant and the lieutenant were somehow supposed to make the tour in combat go as easy as possible. In pursuing their own understanding of the *take care* concept, small unit leaders issued a constant stream of orders that seemed to the troops to make even less tolerable the adversities of life in the bush. Examples of the two *take care* definitions clashing are innumerable, but three were likely to recur daily, and for over a year in the cases of many troops.

The best time of year for conducting search and destroy operations or patrols was also the hottest part of the year in Vietnam. The troops always wanted to leave helmets and flak jackets behind, since they only made a hot day hotter. But with few exceptions small unit leaders always directed that the two items be worn, since they lessened the seriousness of wounds incurred.

A second clash of interest centered on the approved Defense Department methods of combatting malaria and heat casualties — the infamous yellow malaria pills and pink salt tablets. By ordering the pills' consumption, small unit leaders were helping keep their units combat efficient, they were taking care of their men. As far as the troops were concerned however, both pills only made life in the bush more miserable — the former caused diarrhea and the latter nausea, and besides, everybody had a buddy who took both but still became a heat casualty one day and was medevaced with malaria the next.

The third example centered on the occurrence most frequent and frustrating to junior enlisted men both in and out of combat — the word change. In the bush the word change could take forms nearly fatal to morale. A unit might reach an objective hill in the late afternoon and be told by a higher headquarters to spend the night there. The troops would then be told to "dig-in" — to dig foxholes for shelter in case of attack. Digging a hole three or more feet deep was a project costly in strength and patience, but at its completion the distant headquarters might call back and direct still another move before nightfall.

Whatever explanation offered the troops was insufficient — they considered the dig-in directive no more than unnecessary harassment, a make-work project whose only purpose was to prevent their taking a much-deserved rest while the lieutenant or company commander leisurely shot the breeze with the faraway battalion headquarters. The result in the troops' minds was, at least, lingering questions about the sanity of their leaders, and at worst, a growing resentment for which there was no vent. The two unit leaders, however, had ample justification for their dig-in order in the uncertainty inherent in combat — one never knows when "the shit will hit the fan," when the enemy will open fire. They were thus taking care of their troops' lives. And if that wasn't convincing enough, they could always redirect upward the question of the sanity of leaders — the colonel and the general didn't know what was really going on outside their air-conditioned bunkers.

The two different interpretations of the *take care* concept point out a fundamental difference in the outlook of leaders and troops. The former were concerned with the performance of a group; the latter, with one individual. The differences which grew out of such opposite perspectives were virtually irreconcilable and led to a long train of misunderstandings. The leader-trooper relationship was simply not at all conducive to the exercise by either of an empathy for the other which perhaps could have prevented both misunderstandings and fraggings.

Every soldier, marine, sailor or airman who fragged a unit leader believed at the time of the incident that he acted with more than ample justification. Such a view may sound incredible now, but anyone who has seen combat and perceived what it does to one's thinking processes can appreciate the extreme difficulty, perhaps even the folly, of making value judgements on the thoughts and actions of men in a combat environment from a haven now made safe by both time and distance. The assignment of guilt borders on the immoral when made across such differences of perspective. Being within a few weeks or days of a safe exit from so dangerous and unpredictable an environment as the Vietnam War caused one to formulate definitions of terms like "reasonable" and "justified" which he would not make in any other situation.

Explanations offered for the fragging of unit leaders indicated a belief that one's survival was threatened. Two specific and one general type of incident provoked nearly all such assumptions. First, two dates were always in the minds of Americans in Vietnam: R & R and Tour Rotation, one's last day in the Nam. The last thing a trooper wanted to hear was that either of those dates had been changed. In his anxiety to leave the war, he could see no real justification for either of those two dates being "messed with by some paper-shuffling lifer in the rear." Yet these important dates were sometimes changed, often with no explanation to the grunts.

The occurrence of a fragging is even more understandable, though no more justifiable, in the light of a second incident. Normal, though unofficial, practice among field units was to relieve men of patrol responsibilities within a few days of their rotation. Both troops and leaders were aware of the practice and the former naturally looked forward to the few days they could pass out water, C-rations and mail instead of stalking VC or NVA. Occasionally, however, the combat situation dictated that such a policy be set aside. In such cases the troops affected were convinced there was someone around who "didn't like me and wanted to screw me out of some slack time and maybe even get me zapped."

The general variety of incident can be labeled "unnecessary harassment." With their different training, duties and outlook, leaders and troops held as completely different interpretations of unnecessary harassment as they held of the *take care* concept. Examples of unnecessary harassment are nearly infinite in number, but the most frequently and loudly bitched about included making troops: cut their hair, salute and shine their boots in rear-echelon areas; collect and bury all refuse from C-ration meals in the field; carry more weight in the field than the troops felt necessary; improve defensive positions constantly when "any fucking idiot can see the damn hole's good enough — I mean how perfect can you make a damn hole in the ground anyway?"; clean their rifles when they much preferred sleeping, eating or bullshitting with buddies; plus the standard three mind-blowers in the bush, malaria and salt pills, flak jackets and helmets, and the constant word changes. And behind all these things was the fear that they would get stuck with a lieutenant or platoon sergeant who would want to carry out all kinds of crazy John Wayne tactics, who would use their lives in an effort to end the war single-handedly, win the big medal, and get his picture in the hometown paper. In the troops' view, by increasing the unnecessary harassment or by merely allowing it to continue, unit leaders were "pushing too hard where they didn't have to"; they were keeping the troops' lives full of "petty bullshit" which understandably provoked deep anger and resentment in the latter. Some could not deal with such heavy emotions.

The abuse of authority did much to provoke fraggings, and developments far away from Vietnam contributed much to the abuse of authority. Preparations for any war necessitate a rapid increase in the size of an armed force. To meet personnel requirements, standards of recruitment are lowered, and training cycles accelerated. Inevitably the quality of both leaders and troops declines. In addition to the usual wartime attrition by combat casualties, there were two features of the Vietnam War which further accelerated the personnel turnover and thus the decline in quality.

First, by official policy, officers and most NCOs were rarely allowed to keep their combat assignments for more than six months, approximately half the tour of duty in Vietnam. A leader could barely learn his job or get to know his troops before he would be transferred. Field units were thus led by a succession of the inexperienced. Second, anti-war sentiment in the United States grew steadily after the 1965 introduction of American ground forces in the war. With fewer volunteers available, there were far fewer highly-motivated leaders and troops to be recruited in 1968 or 1969 than in 1965. In the fourth and fifth years of the war incidents of abuse of authority became more frequent. There were simply too many leaders who, to cover deficiencies in their own ability, settled on the most Machiavellian methods of leadership in pursuit of their visions of battlefield glory. And there were too many leaders who hid behind smug sentiments like, "they don't have to like what you say — they just have to do it."

Perhaps the most perverse manifestation of the lower quality of small unit leadership was the use of the combat environment as a punishment. Standard practice among field units was to rotate each day the dangerous point, or lead, position on patrols or unit moves; each man could thus project which day he would have point. On occasion, however, certain men were kept on point several days in a row. Such selectees were not kept on point because they possessed any special ability for the duty, but because they had been identified as "troublemakers" by their platoon sergeant or platoon commander. They had probably bitched too much, or were a little slow or lacking in enthusiasm while carrying out an earlier directive. In some cases the abuse was carried even further — a man was kept on point up to the day before he was to leave Vietnam. So malicious and twisted a practice could always, however, be buried under a flood of words about the "situation imposed by the enemy."

In at least one sense, lower ranking elisted personnel not oriented toward a military career contributed more than their leaders to the tragic reality of fraggings — they were the ones who threw or planted the grenades. The overwhelming majority of the troops were not prepared by background, temperament, or intellect for the amount of thinking which would have developed even some understanding of the priorities involved in their leaders' decision-making. They were only prepared to be highly suspicious and resentful of authority figures and those who had been to college, since in the view of most, such people were only "snobs and pricks out to screw a guy." And most troops were prepared to be very selfish in the smallest sense of the term: "It's just like my old man said — a guy's gotta look out for old number one first and all the other turds in the world last."

Bringing the probability of fraggings even closer to reality was a change in the character of the troops' basically self-oriented outlook occurring in the course of a twelve or thirteen-month tour in the combat zone. During the first half of the tour troops were concerned with their own combat efficiency; in the latter half they worried about their own survival first and their combat functioning second. They then had no trouble putting their own well-being above that of the rest of the unit. Therein lay the danger of an attack on another American, for any perceived threat to one's survival of his "year in Hell" was likely to cause him to consider fragging as his only effective recourse. Deep anger and frustration often demand an outlet more satisfying than mere profanity can offer. Those who needed someone to blame for general adversity or for a specific irritation or threat quickly settled on the nearest, the most visible authority figures: "That's it, Man — I'm gonna frag me a lifer some night!"

American servicemen have always bitched about the situation imposed by the enemy as well as the situation imposed by the Pentagon; malaria pills and more word changes were merely new issues to which an old practice was extended. New developments in war appeared in Vietnam and go much farther in explaining fraggings. The percentage of ethnic minorities in the armed forces in the late 1960s was higher than ever before, and reporters suffered less censorship than their predecessors in any previous war.

The Vietnam War was fought by troops coming from a society under-going rapid changes. Most notable was the improved living standard and social position being won by minorities. Troops, white and not, could see the many gains that had been secured by the long train of dramatic acts of protest, and often of violence, which occurred in the 1960s. This is not to imply that minority group members were responsible for the fraggings that occurred in Vietnam; only that the socioeconomic groups from which troops come were more aware than ever before of the lines between classes and the actual power and rights enjoyed by people on different sides of those lines. They were more sensitive than ever before to such ideas as equality, justice and oppression. The psychological condition of some individuals in Vietnam was not at all conducive to their making a rational interpretation of such terms.

Considering the number of troops involved in actual combat operations, an unusually high number of reporters and VIPs were allowed access to the war. In addition to the more professional journalists, there were many young and inexperienced observers overly susceptible to the sensational. With the war largely devoid of big, decisive battles, other kinds of drama had to be looked for. Fraggings, drug abuse and atrocities answered the need; with censorship more relaxed than in previous conflicts, such incidents could be reported immediately to America and the world. What such circumstances meant to the individual trooper — worried most about surviving the war and sensitive about justice and oppression, real or imagined — was that he had available to him the means of projecting himself and his complaint over both his adversity and the entire military hierarchy. By fragging a lifer he could take his case directly to his people over the heads of all the "snobs and pricks out to screw a guy."

There was one major feature of the Vietnam War that was absent from all other wars in which America has been involved. It was a characteristic that explains why the adversity and harassment that have always filled the lives of soldiers were much less tolerable to the Vietnam grunts; it thus explains fraggings more completely than any individual complaint. In spite of hundreds of explanations, exhortations and pleadings from the White House, the objectives of the war were never clearly understood by the grunts who fought it. There was no easily-identified evil to be defeated, as Hitler, Tojo, and Mussolini had personified for an earlier generation.

The lack of a clearly-understood objective helped make the Vietnam grunts the least docile that America has ever put in uniform. The war seemed meaningless to many, especially after the massive Tet offensive by the NVA in 1968, so why should one endure adversity for nothing? Since the troops answered that question in the negative, they refused to tolerate any more than the minimum amount of adversity — and the troops reserved the right to define "minimum." In an environment in which too much of their lives seemed to be in the hands and arbitrary minds of others, deciding when they could tolerate no more adversity — whether or not they would frag a lifer — was the one decision troops reserved for themselves — for dear life, for dear sanity.

Though anger or blame directed at a specific individual might be justified, fraggings never were. It is true that built into the system of the military hierarchy and the different duties it dictated was the means for provoking much resentment and misunderstanding between leaders and troops. But there was not built into that system the means for either making understandable to troops the priorities that caused leaders to make the decisions they made, or for making understandable to leaders the basically different outlook of troops. This lack of proper orientation caused the troops to consider supposedly sound directives merely unnecessary harassment. Whenever such priorities or orientations were understood, it was only the result of a few individuals, leaders and troops, making an extra effort. In most units, more autocratic attitudes prevailed.

During a decade in which authority came under increasingly heavy attack in all fields of activity, a high potential for confrontation between leaders and followers was nurtured. The refusal or inability to lessen that potential in the military, combined with the absence of an easily understood objective in the war, increased the possibility of fraggings. It will never be known exactly how many times the potential became a reality, but one fact will always stand out — such incidents between Americans never occurred with such frequency before the Vietnam War.

14

Reactions

In the months and years since the final American ground patrol was completed in July 1972, the Vietnam veterans have registered a wide variety of reactions to what they saw and did in the war. There were actually as many reactions to the war as there were Americans in it — about two and one-half million. Little understanding results from dividing the two and one-half million into hawk and dove stereotypes or variations of either to describe the war's effects, for even within such arbitrary subdivisions one soon runs into so baffling a variety of reactions that the categories themselves are rendered largely meaningless. The most accurate and realistic thing one can do now is list the reactions to the war that have been manifested thus far. Such a listing may well give some indication of future reactions now only latent.

Many of the ex-grunts returned home proud of what they and their country had done in Vietnam. Many others returned ashamed of their own and their country's connection with Southeast Asian affairs. And still others returned with a wide variety of reactions between pride and shame. Making easier an understanding of the proud is the fact that so many of them have been among the most vocal veterans. The proud veterans freely express the same sentiments they used to put in their letters home; the hope that North Vietnam would be blanketed with atomic bombs or at least invaded and occupied so the people there could be "straightened out." And though they hoped for their own safe return from the war, they could also write that they were willing to stay in the war "as long as there's a VC or NVA that's trying to kill me and my friends and the flag I stand for."

The pride many veterans feel had three major sources. First, they are unshakably convinced that the United States is the greatest country in the world, and they feel privileged to have been given the chance in Vietnam to help keep America the greatest. These veterans believe that one of the best contributions to American greatness is a military contribution.

A second source of pride for many veterans is their admiration for group unity, probably derived from a fear of peer ostracism learned from their parents and schoolmates. They are acutely aware of the fact that they gave their President unquestioned loyalty; they did their part to preserve unity in the execution of America's mission in Vietnam. These veterans consider the willingness to give loyalty to authority figures one of the few valid tests of one's worth to his nation.

Like their parents, the proud veterans hold a deep intolerance for those not sharing their views on the values of giving loyalty and, preserving unity. Some back in the States who did not share those values kept their differing views to themselves. Others felt their dissent should be expressed in a voice loud enough for all to hear. To the proud grunts, the loudmouth hippies back in the World were the most obvious of adversaries — they were guilty of two unforgivable acts. First, by their constant demonstrating they had poisoned the minds of many civilians, thereby preventing the latter from uniting behind the President so the war could be won or at least ended as fast as possible. Second, by their draft card burning and constant screaming, "Ho, Ho, Ho Chi Minh, Viet Cong are gonna win," the hippies had encouraged the North Vietnamese and Viet Cong to fight instead of seeing the light and surrendering. They had thus made the grunts' job of fighting those enemies infinitely more difficult; they had stabbed the grunts in the back. While the grunts had been humping the hills and getting caught in ambushes, the hippies were sitting around with a reefer in one hand and the other on their girl's body, discoursing on the evils of American society and the illusory point at which loyalty ends and treason begins. Small wonder the proud grunts came home aching to "get my hands on one of them fucking hippy-bastards who was hiding behind his college deferment and waving a VC flag while my buddies was getting blowed all to hell, all to hell!"

The third source of pride is the grunts' prewar experiences. A particular combination of experiences allowed the military to take on a deeply personal significance. There are and always have been many for whom the military and war offered the first real opportunity for meaningful association and expression in life. They had rarely had the right answer in class, they had never been invited to parties, they had always been cut from the team, and all that their teachers had been able to come up with was, "George, you must apply yourself more, just apply yourself." Many of these found that when they got to boot camp there were things they could do about which others would say "Wow!" or "Nice going, Georgie." The praise was welcome, intoxicating. In Vietnam it continued, but for much different acts. Expertise in the application of brutality or even killing won the same praise in the war as had 100 pushups in training.

For others the war offered a nice continuation of a kind of expression and recognition they had grown used to. Those who had made the football team back at All-American High School found the same exhilaration from combat exploits — carrying a buddy out of enemy fire or killing Vietnamese — as they had previously found in scoring touchdowns and winning the big game. For them the war offered the chance to live certain illusions they had formulated themselves or had been taught, principally the one that says there is glory in war just like there is in football. They were not at all prepared to hear anyone even hint that in following such an idea they had been chasing a ghost.

Another large number of veterans came home full of shame over what they had seen and done in the war. Some are ashamed of themselves for being part of a group, the Military Assistance Command, Vietnam, that produced so much bitterness and blood, so much disillusion and death, but so little progress and peace. They are surprised and disappointed that they were so easily and thoroughly deceived by the politicians into joining such an enterprise. Others are ashamed in an impersonal way. They are ashamed of what they saw their country doing to another people involved in their own version of the American Revolution.

Like the proud, the ashamed veterans carry some intolerance but it differs from that of the proud in two respects. First, it is directed at those who stood up like robots at the presidential call to arms and those who said anything goes — atrocities, nuclear weapons — in the fight against communism, and second, in it is mixed an element of pity for those they believed misled by the super-patriots. To the ashamed, the protesters were heroes, the gifted vanguard who could see more clearly than the masses the true character of events.

The ashamed have done different things with their reaction. Some want so badly to erase the war from their memories that they don't admit to anyone they were once there. A few of these have enough will power to suppress their shame; they are using whatever routine they adopted on their return to push Vietnam into the distant and fuzzy past of other people. "I'm a different person now — I was never there," says a veteran now helping an uncle manage a resort in Canada. Others who want to erase the memory don't have the will. Whatever they do they can still feel their war experiences hanging swollen in their conscience. They are doing the only thing they can — waiting for time to obscure the sharper corners, the brighter colors of the memory.

Still other veterans who reacted with shame have decided they can do things worthwhile with their shame. For these the war occasioned a new application of the attitude exemplified by James Dean, Martin Luther King, Jr. and the Kennedys — a more just world can be built. War, like segregation and cancer, not only should be eliminated but can be. These veterans have decided to organize and try to explain to the country their revulsion to the war. Though there may be some basis for criticizing some of their methods, the impact on the American news media and public of Vietnam Veterans Against the War is not to be overlooked in any consideration of veterans' activities. VVAW has shown that veterans who prefer peace to war are not spoiled kids throwing tantrums nor are they communist dupes. The activist veterans are concerned young Americans who have identified and are committed to changing certain widespread attitudes that make more possible the occurrence of war; attitudes such as: the President is always right because he is the President, commumism is worth crusading against, and there is glory in war. The activist veterans have succeeded in making many in the working class aware of the inequalities in war and the terrible price of their patriotism — it is their sons who do the dying in wars declared by politicians and acquiesced to by the majority of the population.

One group of veterans is noteworthy for their complete lack of adjustment problems. Their attitudes have been personified as long as there have been big events to batter people around. They are the uncommitted, the uninvolved, and they feel that big events only hurt those who think about them. These veterans figure the Vietnam War was just another of those big and sometimes bloody events that happen to people in the course of life. If such events can be avoided, then fine; but, if not, then one just has to go along with them because "there's not a hell of a lot one guy can do about them things anyway. Hell, Man, war's been happening for thousands of years and they're gonna happen for thousands more. No use fighting it . . . just go and get back as quick as you can, that's about all you can do, right?"

Many more of the ex-grunts could not take the war in stride. They were simply and thoroughly horrified by it, by its bigness and by the mindless way it ran over individuals, feeding on bodies and dreams with no regard for friendship or promises made. Some were horrified because the massive and uncontrolled event that was the war did to them what they would allow no individual or event to do — strip away the veneer of pretense from their own particular weakness and deficiencies. They have carefully selected the memories and interpretations they will allow to survive and be recounted, discarding that which does not reinforce the myth they now cling to in a death grip — the view that they knew exactly what they were doing every step of the way.

These veterans will not let themselves do anything that might convey the slightest hint that they were taken advantage of and used, that they were not astute enough to see through an event of shallow justification, that they were exposed as the character no one wants to be, just another "dumbass peon." Never again will they allow themselves to be lured close to the glare and heat of events in the making, naked of the cushion of time and space such events always wore in high school history classes. As soon as they touched back down on American territory and their discharge was processed, they raced back to the womb-niche from which they had been pried loose either by the draft or visions of glory. Once back in that niche they resolved never to leave it again: "The whole country, the whole fucking world could blow up and I wouldn't lift a finger for them again. I did a good job over there — I know I did — but my thing's right here and I ain't never gonna leave it again, never."

Others were horrified for another reason. They may or may not have been strong in the face of adversity when they went, but they came back broken, for they were presented with a bigger dose of shock than they could assimilate. They are terribly and perhaps permanently confused about the war. They long to understand it so they can build a future above and beyond it, but it took something from them that cannot be quickly or easily replaced — the frame of reference needed to distinguish between the logical and the illogical. Except possibly for the quadriplegics, these veterans are the most tragic victims of the war.

To them, logic looks absurd, absurdity looks logical. They can't make realistic decisions about the future because they are no longer sure what reality is. The war was madness in motion; it was a surrealistic landscape brought to life and yet it was a real historical event, real enough to wrench once solid values out of all recognizable and useful shape. Now for the confused veterans the mad play of life on the planet Earth goes on, bouncing back and forth between reality and illusion, and they feel strapped to a seat before that stage. Action is okay, passivity is okay, brutality is okay, love is okay — they're all okay, they're all worthless, "who gives a shit?"

One final major reaction is probably held by more veterans than any other. Those who hold it are not a group apart from those who hold other reactions to the war — they are for the most part veterans who have reacted with anything but pride. After they had been home for awhile, or during the latter months of their Vietnam tour in some cases, a considerable number of the veterans came to feel they had been lied to and used for a purpose not worth their sweat and blood. Though that number is impossible to determine, I put it at between fifty and seventy-five percent of all the younger generation veterans.

The origin of this fourth reaction probably lies in an attitude widespread among infantrymen in Vietnam after 1968: the grunts of the latter years of the war did not feel they were part of a crusade to save Vietnam from communism. But they did think they were going to do something important, something that would help a less fortunate people, and something that would answer their own human need to find meaning in life.

200

Most believed their national leaders when they said there was a good reason to go, and most understood the implication in the call — the project might not be exactly pleasant. Once in Vietnam, however, that sense of importance began to dissipate. No matter how many patrols they went on, how many air strikes they called, how many rounds they fired at sounds in the night, and no matter how much money they gave to build schools and hospitals, nothing ever got any better. Vietnam stayed as backward and screwed up as it was at the beginning of everyone's tour. The war then became an apolitical and personal project — the struggle to survive it. The only thing the grunts found to win in Vietnam was 365 consecutive days of life.

The politicians had lied, and worse still, they could either never see the war as the grunts saw it or they refused to listen to those who tried to tell them why it could never be won. So most of the smiling, glad-handing public officials continued to deceive the grunts, the grunts' parents, the whole country and worst of all, themselves. To these grunts phrases such as, "honoring our commitments to the South East Asia Treaty Organization," and "Turning back the tide of communist aggression," or "buying time for the South Vietnamese," and fighting on until we can achieve "peace with honor," were all bullshit. The name of the game was survival.

It is obvious not only from this account but the publicized actions of the veterans themselves that the war had a massive effect on the grunts' lives. In many cases it had an even larger effect than that worked by their parents. We don't have to wait decades to judge that the war was the hardest experience the grunts have faced in their lives. For most it will remain the hardest thing they will ever face. The war taught them what they either did not know at all or only suspected before they went — life is full of adversity and it is rarely deserved. There are many ways of learning that lesson, but none of the other ways can teach the lesson as fast and in so direct a manner as war. The Vietnam War invested many young minds with some very old attitudes.

No one can now tell what lasting influences the Vietnam veterans will have on the rest of their generation or what effect the war will have on American society and history, but a few indications already can be discerned. An event as big as war always touches many more than those who wear uniforms and carry arms in it. It occasionally happens that a war provokes a common resolve in those who saw it close up and those who witnessed it from a great distance. The Vietnam War in particular provoked a unity of sorts between the minority of the young generation who went and the majority who did not. Those who were bloodied in the hundreds of demonstrations against the war were also lied to and deceived, and tasted disillusion. They and the veterans have resolved to tolerate less abuse of authority and deception in life than previous generations. They have advanced new answers to old questions: what is the proper role of America and its military machine in international affairs? What is the proper role of force in human relations?

Those born between 1940 and 1954 saw the same gaping contradictions in life every other maturing generation saw, and many of them made the same complaint against official deception and brutality other generations made. But, reformers in the Vietnam generation enjoyed an advantage over their predecessors. They were assisted in making their anti-war/anti-violence case by television — the very instrument that had kept so many of them naive — and a large army of reporters. Thus the peace message received wider dissemination than ever before. And while it also provoked a passionate and sometimes violent opposition, it is now a firmly-established tenet in the lifestyle of millions of Americans.

The Vietnam War was the event which blooded another American generation. It was for them what Bunker Hill, Gettysburg, Belleau Wood, and Guadalcanal were to earlier generations; and like those earlier generations, after the event they too are taking another small degree of inhumanity out of our way of life.

Epilogue

By now most of the Vietnam grunts have found what they consider an acceptable postwar existence. Most have stopped wandering and have either gotten their thing together or made enough progress toward that end that it will soon be reached. They are doing the same things the grunts of other wars have done when they became veterans. They are selling insurance, pumping gas, attending law school, tending bar, raising beef cattle, putting up telephone poles, sorting mail, photographing babies, driving trucks, piloting airplanes, wearing police badges, leaning on air hammers, teaching analytical geometery, laying bricks, polishing caskets, fixing car engines, coaching football, cutting hair, programming computers, growing corn and repairing television sets. And they are doing something else their predecessors did. They are slowly deciding how to answer the question their children will ask in five, ten, fifteen years — what did you do in Vietnam, Dad?

The colors of First Battalion, Third Marine Regiment now wave in the warm Pacific breezes over Pearl Harbor. In the battalion and regimental commanders' offices another campaign streamer hangs from the unit battle standards. The battalion operations staff now issues plans to "advance the state of training" instead of orders to "seek out, close with and destroy the enemy." Advancing the state of training now includes scheduling unit beer parties, classes on drug abuse and venereal disease, practicing for inter-command golf, rifle, and boxing matches, and selecting a command nominee for Military Wife of the Year.

Bravo Company has a new generation of grunts. They have never heard of Captain Sam, Virginia Ridge or Hill 174, and they don't spend their precious liberty time poring through the official histories for such details. They are now doing the same things marines and soldiers have always done after the shooting stops: practicing battlefield tactics they will probably never use, manicuring lawns, polishing everything in sight for the next inspection.

Though the postwar troops are probably not aware of it, links do exist between themselves and the Vietnam grunts. On the walls of all the company recreation rooms hang portraits of those who won the Medal of Honor in Vietnam. The newest grunts, those who will never see the Nam, watch television, shoot pool or check out for weekend home visits and parties under the cold gaze of boyish faces, under the officious descriptions of legendary feats now largely forgotten. "With complete disregard for his own personal safety . . . crossing the fire-swept terrain . . . refused medical attention . . . skillfully maneuvered his squad through dense undergrowth and withering enemy fire . . . silenced the enemy machine guns before succumbing to his own wounds . . . brought credit to himself and his Service . . . in the finest traditions . . . the finest traditions . . . the finest traditions . . . ."